Who Owns the West?

Who Owns the West?

by William Kittredge

MERCURY HOUSE
SAN FRANCISCO

Published in the United States by Mercury House, San Francisco, California, a non-profit publishing company devoted to the free exchange of ideas and guided by a dedication to literary values.

This publication has been supported by a grant from the Walter & Elise Haas Fund.

The author and publisher gratefully acknowledge the following publications, in which portions of the essays in this book were previously published in slightly different form: *Antaeus, Audubon, Big Sky Journal,* British *Vogue, Countryside, Culture, Culture Front, Esquire,* German *Geo, Harper's,* Los Angeles *Times, New Republic, Northern Lights, Outside, Ploughshares,* and *Time.* The excerpt on pp. 67–68 is from Avrahm Yarmolinsky, ed., *The Portable Chekhov.*

United States Constitution, First Amendment: Congress shall make no law respecting an establishment of religion, or prohibiting the free exercise thereof; or abridging the freedom of speech, or of the press; or the right of the people peaceably to assemble, and to petition the Government for a redress of grievances.

Mercury House and colophon are registered trademarks of
Mercury House, Incorporated

Designed by David Peattie. Printed on recycled, acid-free paper.
Manufactured in the United States of America.

Library of Congress Cataloging-in-Publication Data:

Kittredge, William.
White people in paradise : who owns the west / by William Kittredge
p. cm.
ISBN 1-56279-078-1 (acid-free paper)
1. West (U.S)—Description and travel. 2. Natural history—West (U.S.)
3. Conservation of natural resources—West (U.S.) 4. Environmental protection—
West (U.S.) I. Title.
F595.3.K54 1996
978' .03—dc20 95-11058 / CIP

5 4 3 2

For Annick

Who Owns the West?

PROLOGUE

White People in Paradise

On May 14, 1988, I watched a parade of 330 logging trucks, each loaded with fresh-cut timber, head out on a parade through the small country towns of the Bitterroot Valley in Montana—Lolo to Florence, Victor to Hamilton, and on to Darby in the backlands country near the Idaho border. They were hauling 1.5 million board feet of saw-logs to the Darby Lumber Company mill, which was threatening to close (currently it is closed).

Country citizens gathered along the roadside to watch and wave and cheer. Called the Great Northwest Log Haul, that parade got started up the road in northwestern Montana around Libby, where milling logs is not just the major industry but a way of life. It ended sometime after three o'clock in the morning with a street-dance celebration. Hoyt Axton was filming nearby, and he came out to entertain.

Perfectly Western: supporting one another, taking care of their own. You have to respect it.

Along the unpaved back roads in Montana and northern Idaho Day-Glo green signs proclaim: THIS FAMILY SUPPORTED BY THE TIMBER INDUSTRY. This is as much of the world as we've got, such people are saying. Our share, and we mean to keep it.

At a glass-topped table on a brick-floored garden patio behind a posh townhouse in Washington, DC, I found myself talking with people who were, at least in my book, sort of famous and powerful. One was a liberal senator from New England.

They found out I was from Montana, and quizzed me. Why did so many people out there seem to despise our national government? What was their problem? Who were they?

They were talking about the public anger that seems to be surfacing everywhere in the West—gun-packing men on the streets of obscure little towns in Idaho and Montana, dropping hints about revenge if they can't have justice. Revenge for what? What injustices had they suffered?

"They feel disenfranchised," I said, "and powerless."

The people around the table looked impatient. "What do they want?" one of the women said. "It's the same for all of us. Is everybody out there angry? Are they children?"

She seemed angry; I looked away.

Not long ago in the American West it was easy to think we were living in harmony with an inexhaustible paradise. That became, for many, a habit of mind, hard to shake.

But aspects of our paradise have been worked to death. The old-growth timber has been mostly logged; the great salmon runs have vanished; cattle and sheep tromp streamsides to dust and dust again; hard metals percolating up from mine shafts abandoned decades ago poison our mountain waters.

A wave of newcomers is moving in. Popular mythology, trying to name our circumstances, has it that we are overrun with tourists, computer companies, and good Thai restaurants—which is of course not true unless you happen to be in one of the famous resorts, like Aspen or Jackson Hole, or happening towns like Boise or Bozeman, or a chic wayside stop like Ennis, Montana, where you can also get a terrific meal (but not Thai). These new settlers are not just well-to-do citizens making a getaway from the overpopulated insanities of our cities but also refugees out of Mexico and Southeast Asia bringing the enormous energies of the dispossessed. The West is being resettled, again, by people seeking sanctuary and opportunity. Some Native Americans smile and shake their heads. "Now," they say, "It's happening to you."

Again our culture in the West is remixing and reinventing itself. It's a process many locals, descendants of people who came west only a few generations back, have come to hate; some think they own the West because their people suffered for it, and in that way earned it. They feel that it's being taken away from them, and they're often right; they think they are being crowded out, and they are. They feel that nobody in greater America much cares about their well-being or dreams, and they are right.

Westerners, like most people, tend to know themselves through their work. Many mines and lumber mills are closing; ranches are being turned into hunting preserves. Small towns are dying.

The world is moving on in its heedless way, and many Western people feel they are being tricked out of their natural heritage. They feel humiliated by their economic powerlessness; some have come to fear and hate strangers. Many would like to close the gate, lock down the West, and call it their own, forever.

Some have grown deeply paranoid, and band together, forming a spectrum of small political entities; the weakest pity themselves; some like to think they are warriors, defending their society; others are insane in their anger. Some sad creature—not necessarily a Westerner—was perhaps driven by feelings such as these to detonate the bomb that killed those children and adults in Oklahoma City.

What to do, besides brood on the ultimate unfairness of things? Sometimes I am moved to drive with Beethoven's Archduke Trio playing over and over like glory as I exceed speed limits and swing wide through the long curves, plunging into and out of flickering shadows of the fir trees, trying to shake thoughts of mortality, of what's to become of us.

Despair, the music tells me, is a useless way of connecting to the world. Slow down, it tells me, and love what there is.

Not long ago, in a fit of such traveling, on my way to Seattle, I took a rest stop in a little town out in the vastness of eastern Washington between Spokane and Wenatchee. As I paid for my provisions a wiry, balding little man, tossing a huge set of keys from hand to hand, was joking and talking to the cashier, a plump woman with vivid red hair who seemed to be an old pal, maybe even a sister or a once-upon-a-time lover.

The balding man said, glancing at me as he tossed his keys one last time, "These women won't ever help a man unload his truck."

The red-headed woman laughed as the balding man eased off toward the back door, as if what he'd said had been slightly scatological. I had Beethoven on my mind.

Then she turned the glow of her smile directly onto me. "Isn't he something?" she said. "He's one of those boys."

They had been enjoying themselves. We're not all angry. I've know Westerners who liked to drink a little gin and make love in the sweet new-grown clover under a yellow moon.

Who owns the West? All of us, of course. That's the simple answer, which is sort of beside the point when we get down to considering questions of fairness. Stay joyous under the sun and moon, in the rain and out; that's another halfway answer.

Westerners, like everyone, must work to understand that anger looks nowhere but backward, and that this particular variety is ultimately nostalgic and pretty much useless. As anywhere, in the West people—out-of-work redneck timber-fallers and stockbrokers and lady veterinarians, laughing boys, dancing ladies, all of us—have no choice but to reimagine and embrace the future.

PART ONE

Heaven on Earth

1

Our ideas of paradise, it is said, originate in childhood. Mine connect to a great valley out in the deserts of southeastern Oregon, just at the time World War II was beginning. We moved to a huge new ranch, and my father built us a house that was fresh and clean and smelled of sawdust. From the screened veranda we could see out over the wild-hay meadows and willow-lined sloughs of the Thompson Field and beyond to swamplands my father was draining to farm. But fields and farming did not interest me then.

In mid-May, when the old homesteader's apple orchard back of our house was blossoming and thick with mystery, it was time for my father to plant his garden. This was an important venture, meant to help feed his harvest crew. A hired man dumped a horse-drawn plow and a disc and a harrow out of a pickup truck, and the next morning showed up leading a harnessed team of bay geldings. When the soil was worked to a perfect tilth, at least in this memory, my father showed up with stakes and a roll of white twine and began laying out the long precise crop rows.

We were all out there in that vivid spring light—my brother and I, and my mother with my brand-new sister wrapped in blankets. But my father didn't pay us much attention. This was business. He was intent on accuracy, sighting down the strings, setting out six one-hundred-foot rows of strawberries (enough to keep us in crates of strawberries through a long run of summers), onion sets, and corn in hills, as well as peas, pole beans, and squash, all in prelude to the communality of bunkhouse meals. We loved him and one another, but we were spectators. Don't go running through the rows of planted spinach and chard or you will get your butt paddled. It is possible to think of that time as an initiation into the values of distance and order.

The times I recall as sacred came later in the summer. They were sacred because they were useful, encouraging me to love my life, the wonders of the place where I lived, and the possibility in the creature that I was. Our irrigation ditch wove through a a couple of miles of sandy hills from a low dam in Deep Creek Canyon. A long row of old Lombardy poplar creaked and rustled in the afternoon winds while I sat on my heels and studied the water flowing through the miniature redwood weirs (called boxes) my father had built in the little ditches across the head end of the garden. The water turned rainbows in the light and muddied in the dry ditch rows and went where it had to go, soaking and seeping. I watched long-legged spiders walk on water. The squash blossomed, yellow-jackets hummed at their business, the corn grew until it was taller than I was, I stole strawberries from under the leaves and stepped on the stink-bug beatles, crushing them and enjoying their stench.

But things had changed by the time I was enrolled up at the one-room Adel School. My brother and sister and cousins and I built play-time ditches and levee banks around little bare-dirt square fields we laid out with what we saw as grown-up precision beneath the apple trees outside the back door to our house. We farmed with toys in the place of the D-7 Caterpillar tractors my father used in his operations out on the far side of the valley. We were preparing for life, imitating what we understood as real.

I was on my way to becoming a little agribusiness farmer.

2

In those long-gone days the highland desert country of south-eastern Oregon was an enclave of unsettled territory, lava rock and sagebrush flats, fault-block mountains, and swampland valleys echoing with the call of white pelicans and Sand Hill Cranes and Canada geese and thousands of ducks, like the green-winged teal and the redheads and canvasbacks nobody sees so often anymore. In such country, expansiveness of the personality was commonplace. Children grew up addicted to running horses, as I did, a manifestation of high spirits that adults claimed to see as a disease to be cured (even if they themselves once in a while staged a race). A running horse, I was told, was not a toy.

We came of age understanding that horses were creatures with their own complex sensibilities, which could not only be broken (that terrible name for training) but spoiled—ruined—by cheap-shit frivolity such as pointless galloping—a boy coming heedlessly down along a country road with his horse in a lather.

But we were the children of people who owned ranches, and could sometimes get away with things, so I listened to what I was told but galloped anyway, down long secret lanes through the willows and sloughs, before sunup in the endlessness of midsummer, on my way to visit the hay camps where the old men in the round corrals were lassoing their teams.

Then, in 1940, the summer I turned nine years old, an older cousin and I were deemed big enough to be useful, and we were sent to ride with my grandfather's crew of buckaroos on the vast sea of deserts east of the ranch, where our family summered several thousand mother cows. We began this serious education under the boss of the buckaroos, a legendary horseman, Ross Dollarhide (everybody knew the story of how he'd ridden to the White Horse Ranch on a fat-tired bicycle, sixteen years old and looking for his first cowhand job, and how he'd ridden a tough horse to death that long-ago morning; his abilities had gone unquestioned ever since).

What a thing it was to be a frightened child, watching Dollarhide step onto some spooky stocking-footed traveling horse in the light of early morning, knowing you were expected to keep up with him for the rest of the day.

For a long time my cousin and I weren't much use to anybody, that summer and most of the next (I was learning to do things like never cry); then we grew and toughened as boys will. By 1943 we were, we thought, almost cowhands. We learned to shoe our own horses, and braid rawhide on rainy days, and travel like grown-ups, at a long trot. We were close to the end of secret galloping; we were becoming little men.

But you have to stay playful to survive. That was another thing we were taught, by clear example, watching the men around us, in whom a certain childish recklessness (at least in the best of them, the finest hands) had never died.

Then that playfulness got us crossways with old man Dollarhide. Just at daybreak one bright morning in June while we were rolling our beds, making ready to move the four-horse chuck wagon from the mountainside camp at Ackley to Sagehen Springs, my cousin and I were detailed to help the wrango boy move the seventy-some saddle horses in the MC remuda. Once we'd turned them out of the willow corral at Ackley they'd be ours as we herded them twenty miles down country across the alkaline flats to the fenced-in field where the wet-weather creek at Sagehen got lost in tall brush. There wasn't much at Sagehen, no sign of a house, just a hog-wire corral and field built of rusty barbed wire and crooked juniper posts. That corral was a small target in a vast territory (nowadays there's a highway called Winnemucca-to-the-Sea just south of Sagehen Springs; in those days there weren't any internal combustion engines in that almost empty country).

Dollarhide told us to take it easy. What we were to do was graze the herd on Ackley Mountain through the morning, and then ease them on down to Sagehen in the late afternoon.

Dollarhide made it real clear: If we got those horses running with their heads, and lost them, there wasn't a fence to turn them within fifty miles. As an afterthought Dollarhide sent along a man named Merle Dodson, to keep an eye on us.

What is there to say about Merle Dodson? He was known as "Tarzan," a barroom tag given him because he was, according to my father when I asked him years later, close to an animal if he was drinking, huge-handed and barrel-chested, stronger than he knew, impossible to wound, nobody to fight as strangers had found out any number of times, but willing and happy to be entertained.

"That damned Tarz," people would say. "If he ain't something, you tell me, what is?"

What he was on this day was full of vinegar when we eased our drifty grazing herd of bay horses, all of them geldings, over the crest of Ackley Mountain to encounter the mustangs who were also drifting along in their shaggy, spotted-horse way.

There were twenty or so mustangs, mares and colts, a half dozen branded geldings that had got away from some ranch in the long-ago past, and no doubt a stud horse even if I don't recall any such creature. What I recall is the way we let them drift into the remuda and mix, the way we fell in after them; I recall running horses.

"We're going to go mustanging," Tarz Dodson whispered. Something like that. It was his plan. It frightened us, but we never thought of refusing.

Besides, if I learned something that day, which is the point of this story, it had nothing to do with caution but rather with the splendor of running with the wind. That was the lesson of the summer.

We were going to ease our great herd of horses along the road slow as we could through the afternoon, then stir them into a long run just at the end, and turn them into corral at Sagehen Springs before they came to any sense of what was happening. We were going to have those mustangs inside fences before they realized they had been trapped.

We were going to own those mustangs. That was Tarz Dodson's idea; the whole buckaroo crew could turn some money on the side. It wasn't a plan my grandfather or Ross Dollarhide would have endorsed.

(I have no memory of what those remnant animals were worth at that time. Their herds grew during WW II, when their natural predators, the young able-bodied cowhands, were off to war. After the war the wild mustangs were cleaned out of that country, run with airplanes and rounded up in great swirling herds; most of them were eventually shot and processed into chicken feed).

We brought it off, my cousin and I and the MC wrango boy and Tarz Dodson, we got the mustangs running with the remuda, we circled our herd in a great sweep through the afternoon while somebody got the corral gate open at Sagehen. It was about then that I realized something was very wrong.

The chuck wagon tent was up, and everybody on the crew but us had turned his horse loose into the field. Which meant our worn-out horses were it; lose the herd and everybody was sort of afoot. Which was no joke in that country, sure as hell not in a buckaroo outfit. Old man Dollarhide was standing out in front of that chuck wagon tent with a coffee cup in his hand, studying our performance with amazement, looking like an old eagle contemplating a final kill.

The rest of what I recall doesn't take long to tell. We hit that corral gate perfectly; those mustangs circled maybe twice, then went right out the other side, scattering hog-wire; they circled in the little field a time or two and went right on through that fence at a long run, the MC remuda following, horses flowering out into their freedom and starting to spill off in all directions, still running, and nothing we could do because we were still back trying to get through the corral gate.

What I remember is somebody, maybe old man Dollarhide himself, took my horse, leaping up into my short-legged saddle, and somebody took my cousin's horse, and the wrango boy's horse.

What had seemed like play ended abruptly. I remember that it was hours before those men came back driving a remnant of the remuda before them. This was a serious disgrace; the MC buckaroo crew was going to be the laughingstock of the country. There for a moment Ross Dollarhide was left afoot, without a horse. I think he thought we had made him look like a fool.

What I think I remember is the silence while we went on standing around the cook fire. Maybe Tarz Dodson was fired and rode off into the night. I don't know.

But what matters most in this memory is the feeling I took away from the moments we turned those running horses in that long sweep outside the corral at Sagehen Springs while somebody opened the gate. It was a kind of pleasure Dollarhide no doubt knew more intimately than I ever would.

Maybe we disgraced his buckaroo crew; maybe I got my ass whipped. I don't think so; I don't think old man Dollarhide ever touched me; he taught me to never actually give a shit about small change; it's been an operative principle with me in my good moments ever since. I'd been along for a big ride, and part of a story that would be told for years, and in that if nothing else I was like Dollarhide, who was the real thing all his life.

In 1848, after service in the Mexican War, a young medical doctor from Virginia named Hugh Glenn began driving great herds of cattle over the difficult trails from the Midwest to the vast inland valleys of California. In time Hugh Glenn was able to establish himself on a Spanish land-grant ranchero near the present-day town of Willows on the Sacramento River.

I went by his home place on a narrow Glenn County road

along the levee above the riverbank about a dozen years ago. All that was left was a driveway lined with exotic imported palms and flowering shrubs. His mansion, the long verandas overlooking the vast fields, and the barns were gone.

I was interested in Glenn because he had great influence in the high desert country of southeastern Oregon. The spring of 1872, free grazing land in California mostly claimed, Glenn turned 1200 shorthorn cows over to a twenty-three-year-old cowhand named Peter French. He sent French, seven *vaqueros*, and a Chinese cook north into mostly unmapped territory in the Great Basin to find new ranchlands.

The Chinese cook was named Charlie On Long. He stayed with French until he was killed in the Bannock uprising of 1878. The *vaqueros*, Vincenti Ortega, Juan Ortega, Jesus Charris, Joquim Berdugo, Francisco Carataguey, Juan Charris, Prim Ortega—some of their nicknames were Tebow, Chino, Chico—lived out their lives in that country; they were legendary in the cow camps in my part of the world, fifty years ago, when I was a child and knew old men who had known them.

Pete French led them up the Pit River, across the Warner Range into Surprise Valley, almost on the Nevada border, north across the southern fringes of Warner Valley where I grew up, and across the high deserts south of the Beatty Buttes, to camp in Catlow Valley below the long western slope of the great 10,000-foot fault block that is Steens Mountain. They were in an almost empty, forgotten enclave in the West, mostly passed by in the rush to settlement in the coastal valleys of California and Oregon.

Other than Shoshoni natives, there was John Devine and

his blooded racing stock over at the Whitehorse Ranch, trappers camped at the Sod House on the southern edge of Malheur Lake, and the military at Fort Harney. The rest of that huge territory was unclaimed by whites except for miners at Silver City, Idaho, and the railroad down south at Winnemucca. Our frontier was closing on its remnants as Peter French drove Glenn's cattle into the oasis valley that he made into his true home in the world.

The long string of that herd came down through the breaks south of the Beatty Buttes and out onto bunch-grass country in Catlow Valley while the long ridge of Steens Mountain there to the cast was still bright with snow. French had been on the trail two months, and tiny yellow and orange flowers bloomed amid the lava rocks and stunted sage.

At Roaring Springs along the western base of the Steens they rested the cattle on good grazing and water. French bought his brand with a few head of cows from a drifter named Porter, a huge P on the left hip, the first thing French was to own in Oregon.

The next morning before daybreak, according to the legends, French rode out of Catlow Valley, over the ridge to the north, and looked down on the great wetland valley of the Donner und Blitzen River for the first time. Those fine meadows were for the taking, and Pete French took them. He fit into that part of the world like a lost piece in a puzzle.

It's easy to imagine that morning was the beginning of his manhood as French would understand it, alone in the boulders and brush, looking down into the enclosed reach of swampy willow-lined sloughs and meadows that lay in the land-locked valley below the rimrocks. Above him lay the high rangelands of the Steens, where the summer grass would never fail. All of it was enclosed by an immensity of sagebrush desert, a buffer against outsiders.

It's easy to imagine snow-geese, the sounds of their wings as he saw the place, knowing it was his, all that he could see, the creekside reach of high ground where he would build his white house and his barns and the willow corrals and, spreading all around, the finest ranching property in the West.

The great landholders like Peter French were, for a long time, the people we imagined when we imagined kings of the mountain in my part of America. But they turned out, I think, to be living inside the wrong dream—they found a paradise, they thought it could be theirs; they yearned to possess it, but their generosities dissolved before that yearning. For a long time we believed in their pomp and their circumstance; we revered them. It was a mistake.

Westerners should revere hay-camp cooks and school teachers and florists and buckaroos and barbers and habadashers. They did endless work, they took care, they were the people who invented our civilization; theirs was a tradition of civility.

Those men who came north with French, the first buckaroos in that country—Tebo, Chino, and Chico—horseback artists who brought the rawhide *riata* and the Spanish silver-sided bits, quick-handed men who never dreamed they could own much beyond a saddle and a bedroll and a good pocketknife, they were our nobility; like old man Dollarhide, I think, they dreamed of capabilities and beauty. They knew better than to imagine you could ever own anything beyond a coherent self.

Those men, and the men I rode with on those deserts when I was a boy, lived in an ancient horseback world that is mostly gone. The nineteenth century lasted in our part of the universe until the spring of 1946, when my grandfather traded off some two hundred matched work teams for a fleet of John Deer tractors. Everybody thought it was a bold step into the future. We didn't know what we were losing, our ancient proximity with animals, with running horses. The shadows of clouds went on swiftly without us.

3

A scab-handed wandering child who rode off on those old horses, I grew up with the constant thronging presence of animals. Herds of feral hogs inhabited the swampland tule beds where the waterbirds nested. Those hogs would eat the downy young of the Canada geese if they could, but they never caught them so far as I knew.

Warner Valley, tucked against that enormous reach of Great Basin sagebrush and lava-rock desert, was a hidden world. The landlocked waters flow down from the snowy mountains to the west but don't find a way out to the sea. They accumulate and evaporate in shallow lakes named Pelican, Crump, Hart, Stone Corral, and Bluejoint.

Sandhill cranes danced their courtship dances in our meadows. The haying and feeding and the cowherding work couldn't have been done without the help of the horses. We could only live the life we had with the help of horses.

All day some Sundays in the summer my family would spread blankets by Deep Creek or Twenty-Mile Creek, and even us kids would catch all the rainbow trout we could stand.

What I want to get at is our isolation. We were thirty-six gravel-road miles over the Warner Mountains from the little lumbering and rancher town of Lakeview (maybe 2,500 souls). Warner Valley was not on the route to anywhere.

The way in was the way out. The deserts to the east were traced with wagon-track roads over the salt-grass playas and around rimrocks from spring to spring, waterhole to waterhole, but nobody ever headed in that direction with the idea of going toward the future.

To the east lay deserts and more deserts. From a ridge above our buckaroo camp beside the desert spring at South Corral, we could see the long, notched, snowy ridge of Steens Mountain off in the eastern distances, high country where whores from Burns went in summer to camp with the sheepherders amid aspen trees at a place called Whorehouse Meadows, where nobody but wandering men ever went, men who would never be around when you needed them. And beyond, toward Idaho, there was more desert.

By the end of the Second World War my grandfather had got control of huge acreages in Warner, and my father was making serious progress at draining the swamplands. The spring of 1946 my grandfather traded off close to two hundred work teams for chicken feed. That is when he replaced those horses with a fleet of John Deere tractors. Harness rotted in the barns until the barns were torn down.

I wonder if my father and his friends understood how irrevocably they were giving up what they seemed to care about more than anything when they talked of happiness—their lives in conjunction to the animals they worked with and hunted. I wonder why they acted like they didn't care.

Maybe they thought the animals were immortal. I recall those great teams of work horses running the hayfields in summer before daybreak, their hooves echoing on the sod as we herded them toward the willow corral at some haycamp, the morning mists, and how the boy I was knew at least enough to know he loved them and that this love was enough reason to revere everything in sight for another morning.

Those massive horses were like mirrors in which I could see my emotions reflected. If they loved this world, and they seemed to, with such satisfaction, on those mornings when our breaths fogged before us, so did I.

Soon after WW II, electricity from Bonneville Power came to Warner, and telephones that sort of functioned. The road over the mountains and down along Deep Creek was paved. Our work in the fields had in so many ways gone mechanical. Eventually we had television. Our isolation was dissolving.

About the time I watched the first Beatles telecast in the early 1960s, Chamber of Commerce gentlemen in Winnemucca got together with like-minded gentlemen from Lakeview and decided it made great economic sense to punch a highway across the deserts between those two little cities. Think of the tourists.

The two-lane asphalt ran north from Winnemucca to Denio, then turned west to cross the million or so acres of rangeland we leased from the Bureau of Land Management, the BLM (we saw those acreages as ours, as if we owned them; in those days we virtually did), over the escarpment called the Dougherty Slide, across Guano Valley and down Greaser Canyon, and directly through our meadowlands in Warner Valley.

I recall going out to watch the highway building as it proceeded, the self-important recklessness of those men at their
work, the roaring of the D-8 Caterpillars and the clouds of dust
rising behind the huge careening of the self-propelled scrapers,
and I recall being excited, sort of full up with pride because the
great world was at last coming to us in Warner Valley. Not that
it ever did. The flow of tourism across those deserts never
amounted to much. But maybe it will, one of these days.

Enormous changes were sweeping the world. We didn't
want to encounter hippies or free love or revolutionaries on the
streets in Lakeview. So we said. But like anybody, we yearned to
be in on the action, we wanted to have our say-so.

Around that time—this may be an apocryphal story, but the
point is we believed it and loved it—a man from the BLM
walked out into a hayfield to give some old rancher an earful
about running too many cattle on his allotment. The rancher
took after him with a gun. The chase led through the fields
until the fellow from the BLM climbed up into a stack of loose
meadow hay, and hid. The old rancher lit the haystack afire.
"Cooked that sonofabitch," the old rancher would say, at least
according to the way I heard the story. It was clearly us against
them.

We were delighted, one Fourth of July, to hear that the
Hell's Angels motorcycle gang from Oakland had headed across
the deserts north to Winnemucca on their way to a weekend of
kicking ass in Lakeview, and that they had been turned back by
a single deputy sheriff.

There had been the long string of lowriders coming on the
two-lane blacktop across one of the great desert swales, and the
deputy, all by himself, standing there by his Chevrolet.

The deputy, a slight, balding man, had flagged down the leaders and they'd had a talk. "Nothing I can do about it," the deputy said, "but they're sighting in their deer rifles. These boys, they mean to sit back there three hundred yards and shoot you off them motorcycles. They won't apologize or anything. You fellows are way too far out in the country."

According to legend, the leaders of the Hell's Angels decided the deputy was right: they knew they were way too far out in the country, and they turned back. I never talked to anybody who knew if that story was true, but we loved it.

It was a story that told us we were not incapable of defending ourselves, or powerless in a nation we understood to be going on without us. We never doubted some of our southeastern Oregon boys would have shot those Hell's Angels off their bikes. Some places were still big and open enough to be safe from outsiders.

During the great flood in December of 1964, when the Winnemucca-to-the-Sea highway acted like a dam across the valley, backing up water over four or five thousand acres, my brother Pat walked a D-7 Caterpillar out along the asphalt and cut the highway three or four times, deep cuts so the floodwaters could pour through and drain away north. What he liked best, Pat said, was socking that bulldozer blade down and ripping up that asphalt with the yellow lines painted on it. We were still our own people.

But even as huge and open to anything as southeastern Oregon may have seemed in those old days, it was also inhabited by spooks. In autumn of the same year the Winnemucca-to-the-Sea highway came across our meadowlands, I had our heavy equipment, our Carry-All scrapers and D-7 bulldozers, at work on a great diversion canal we were cutting through three hundred yards of sage-covered sand hills at the south end of Warner, rerouting Twenty-Mile Creek.

Soon we were turning up bone—human bones, lots of them. I recall a clear October afternoon and all those white bones scattered in the gravel, and my catskinners standing there beside their great idling machines, perplexed and unwilling to continue. Ah, hell, never mind, I said. Crank'em up.

There was nothing to do but keep rolling. Maybe bones from an ancient Indian burial ground were sacred, but so was our work, moreso as I saw it. My catskinners threatened to quit. I told them I'd give them a ride to town, where I'd find plenty of men who would welcome the work. My catskinners didn't quit. I ducked my head so I couldn't see, and drove away.

If you are going to bake a cake, you must break some eggs. That was a theory we knew about. We thought we were doing God's work. We were cultivating, creating order and what we liked to think of as a version of Heaven on Earth.

What a pleasure that work was, like art, always there, always in need of improving, doing. It's reassuring, so long as the work is not boring, to wake up and find your work is still going on, your tools still in the tunnel. You can lose a life in the work. People do.

But we left, we quit, in a run of family trouble. I have been gone from farming and Warner for twenty-five years. People ask if I don't feel a great sense of loss, cut off from the valley and methods of my childhood. The answer is no.

Nothing much looks to have changed when I go back. The

rimrock above the west side of the valley lies as black against the sunset light as it did when I was a child. The topography of my dreams, I like to think, is still intact.

But that's nonsense. We did great damage to the valley as we pursued our sweet impulse to create an agribusiness paradise. The rich peat ground began to go saline, the top layer just blew away. We drilled chemical fertilizers along with our barley seed, and sprayed with 2-4-D Ethyl and Parathion (which killed even the songbirds). Where did the waterbirds go?

But the waterbirds can be thought of as part of the *charismatic megafauna*. Everybody worries about the waterbirds. Forms of life we didn't even know about were equally threatened.

Catostomus warnerensis, the Warner sucker, is threatened. So are three other fish species in the region (three more are endangered, as are two plant species) and riparian tree communities of black cottonwood, red-osier dogwood, and willow.

As a child I loved to duck down and wander animal trails through dense brush by the creeksides, where ring-necked Manchurian pheasants and egg-eating raccoons and stalking lynx cats traveled. Maybe I was often among them, curled in the dry grass and sleeping in the sun, and didn't know it.

The way we built canals in our efforts to contain the wildness of the valley and regulate the ways of water to our own uses must have been close to absolutely destructive to the Warner sucker, a creature we would not have valued at all, slippery and useless, thus valueless. It's likely I sent my gang of four D-7 Caterpillar bulldozers to clean out the brush along stretches of creekside thick with red osier dogwood and black cottonwood.

Let in some light, let the grass grow, feed for the livestock, that was the theory. Maybe we didn't abandon those creatures in Warner, mostly we destroyed them before we left. We did enormous damage in the thirty years that we were there. Country like the Dordogne and Umbria and Tuscany, which has been farmed thousands of years, looks to be less damaged. But maybe that's because the serious kill-off there took place so long ago.

Late in the summer of 1943 I turned eleven out on those high sagebrush and lavarock deserts with my grandfather's cowhand crew. We went at our work in old ways, horseback from daylight until the work was done, riding out from a chuck wagon, changing camp every day, looking after my family's cattle on several hundred thousand acres of rangeland we thought of as ours. We were eating dust with our handkerchiefs tied over our faces like movie cowhands, moving a thousand head of mother cows and spring calves, heading them in toward the ranch, where there was water. The desert had dried up in the last weeks. The overgrown banks of wet-weather creeks were tromped to dust, classical riparian damage which would lead to gully-washing in the spring.

Buckaroos never carried drinking water. Any giving in to the difficulties of the country was a sure sign of weakness. A kid who yearned to be a cowhand would keep his thirst to himself.

What I recall most vividly from those brutal days is the afternoon I got down off my horse and drank what I knew could be piss from a cow's track in muddy ground alongside a dried up seep spring in West Road Gulch on the north side of the

Beatty Buttes. The old hands grinned. I thought to hell with you.

The point I'm trying to make has to do with loving a place because the story of your life is partways located in that place. I won't forget West Road Gulch.

I love Warner as a child loves its homeland, and some sense of responsibility for what's there stays with me. Or maybe I'm just trying to feel good about myself.

But that's what we all want to do, isn't it? It's my theory that everyone yearns, as we did in Warner, plowing those swamps, with all that bulldozing, to make a positive effect in the world. But how?

How to keep from doing harm? Sometimes that seems to be the only question. But we have to act. To do so responsibly we must first examine our desires. What do we really want?

A few years ago I went to Warner with a couple of film-makers from NBC. Some footage ran on the "Today" show. Sitting in an antique GMC pickup truck alongside a great reef of chemically contaminated cowshit that had been piled up out-side the feedlot pens where our fattening cattle had existed like creatures in a machine, I found it in myself to say the valley should be given back to the birds, and turned into a wildlife refuge.

It was a way of saying good-bye. I was saying the biological health of the valley was more important to me than the well-being of the community of ranchers who lived there. I had gone to grade school with some of them. It was an act people living in Warner mostly understood as betrayal.

Some eggs were broken, but I had at last gotten myself to

say what I believed. Around 1990, when I heard that our ranch in Warner, along with two others out in the deserts to the east, was for sale, and that the Nature Conservancy was interested, I was surprised by the degree to which I was moved and excited.

A huge expanse of territory was involved, 1,111,587 acres in an intricate run of private, BLM, and state lands. This included wetlands in the Warner Valley, the Malhuer National Wildlife Refuge (380,000 ducks, 19,000 geese, and 6,000 lesser sandhill cranes migrate through Warner and the Malhuer), the Hart Mountain Wildlife Refuge, the Sheldon National Wildlife Refuge in northern Nevada, and alpine habitats on Steens Mountain, the largest fault-block mountain in North America, with alpine aspen groves and great glacial cirques 3,000 feet deep and twenty miles in length (an area often mentioned as a possible national park).

Maybe, I thought, this would be a second chance in my true heartland, an actual shot at reimagining desire.

What did I really want? A process, I think, everybody involved—ranchers and townspeople, conservationists—all taking part in that reimagining. I wanted them to each try defining the so-called land of their heart's desiring, the way they would have things if they were running the world. I wanted them to compare their versions of paradise, and notice again the ways we all want so many of the same things—like companionship in a community of people we respect, and meaningful work.

Then I wanted them to get started on the painstaking work of developing a practical plan for making their visions of the right life become actual, a plan for using, restoring, and preserving the world I grew up in. I liked to imagine some of the pumps and dikes and headgates would be torn out in Warner, and that some of the swamps would go back to tules. That's part of my idea of progress—recreate habitat for the waterbirds, and the tiny, less charismatic creatures. But nothing like that has happened.

The Nature Conservancy did not end up buying the land. The MC Ranch, our old property in Warner Valley, was stripped of livestock and machinery, and sold to what I understand to be a consortium of local ranchers. I have no idea of their plans—they don't confide in me, the turncoat.

But the world is inevitably coming to Warner Valley. The BLM recently purchased thousands of acres of prime hayland in north Warner, and included it in a special management unit in which no grazing is allowed. The idea of the federal government buying land and taking it out of production (out of the tax base) was unthinkable when I lived in Warner.

Other unthinkable ideas are blowing in the wind. In May 1991, a consortium of environmental groups led by the Oregon Natural Resources Council announced their plan for southeastern Oregon. It included the national park on Steens Mountain, three new national monuments, forty-seven wilderness areas totaling more than 5 million acres, an expanded Hart Mountain Refuge to include the wetlands in Warner Valley, a new National Wildlife Refuge at Lake Albert, wild and scenic river status for fifty-four streams totaling 835 miles (mostly creeks in the glacial cirques in the Steens and Pueblo Mountains), and the phasing out, over a ten-year period, of all livestock grazing on federal lands designated national park, preserve, wildlife refuge, wilderness, or wild and scenic river (about 5.9 million acres).

There's no use sighting in the scopes on deer rifles, not any more. The world is coming to the West, and this invasion will not be frightened away. There is not a thing for the people in my old homeland to do but work out some accommodation.

So many of our people, in the old days of the American West, came seeking a fold in time, a hideaway place where they and generations after them could be at home. Think of *familia*, place and hearth and home fire, the fishing creek where it falls out of the mountains, into the valley, and the Lombardy poplar beside the white house, and the orchard where children run in deep sweet clover under the blossoming apple trees. But that's my old happy place, at least as I remember it, not yours.

We have taken the West for about all it has to give. We have lived like children, taking and taking for generations, and now that childhood is over.

It's time we gave something back to the natural systems of order that have supported us, some care and tenderness, which is the most operative notion, I think—tenderness. Our isolations are gone, in the West and everywhere. We need to give some time to the arts of cherishing the things we adore, before they simply vanish. Maybe it will be like learning a skill: how to live in paradise.

4

If heartaches were commercials we'd all be on TV.

—John Prine

In his late thirties my father had the good fortune to control a huge untouched farming property, a marshland of peat soils that had been building over thousands of years. Such places do not exist any more. He got his hands on a heaven of waterbirds and fertility; he remade it into what he understood as useful, a sprawling system of irrigation and drainage canals, and agribusiness fields where the undulating drillrows ran straight for miles.

He went at it with great energy; he built hundreds of redwood headgates that would never rot; he bought Caterpillar tractors and ran them day and night. People said he was crazy; he was rewarded with legendary crops. He made a lot of money on oats during World War II; he bought racehorses and a Beechcraft Bonanza. Actors and politicians showed up for the hunting. He bought Usher's Scotch by the pickup load. But the governor of Oregon died when the Bonanza went down in the November twilight of 1943; the peat blew and burned and went saline; waterbirds started frequenting some other flyway. After we sold out in 1967 my father retired to the Oregon coast. He fished for salmon and smoked his pipe and kept an eye on the tides.

He was descended from people who took what they wanted, and who understood themselves as a natural ruling class. They were absolutely sure they deserved what they got; they had worked for it; they sacrificed and cared for themselves and their people; they were pitiless in their ability to despise weakness in strangers.

I wonder what my father saw in his most secret sight of the right life. It's my guess he wanted to live out his life surrounded by friends and children and fertile fields of his own designing. I think he wanted to die believing he had been in on the creation of a good sweet place.

Those old pilgrims believed stories in which the West was a promise, a faraway place where decent people could escape the wreckage of the old world and start over. Come to me, the dream whispers, and you can have one more chance.

We like to claim the West is a place where you can have a shot at being what you want to be. You can come to terms with yourself. Freedom, in a livable community, is supposed to be the point of things. It's our prime mythology, and it sort of works out, moreso if you're white and have some money.

Men like my father, and the women who shared their ambitions, were our aristocracy. They are mostly dead. The West they left us is partway ruined, many of our enterprises are a considerable distance out on the rocks, and many of us are somewhat bewildered and heartbroke.

We learned to name ourselves in what we took to be the nobility of their story. But they left us a society that's semi-functional at best. Up the Clark Fork River from the place where I live in Missoula, the Milltown Dam holds six and a half tons of sediment thick with toxic metals from the good old mining days in Butte. Our mountains erode under clear-cut logging, our farm towns are dying, we suffer the whims of a boom-or-bust economy, a history of semi-genocidal racism, and a good-old-boys class system (we love to imagine we are enormously egalitarian, yet so many of us are powerless in any operative sense). And we're always broke.

But we still listen to old promises in the wind. This time, we think, we'll get it right. And we'd better. We've about used up our chances. Like a house cat, the West has only got so many lives.

5

So as a young man I farmed my father's barley fields, running water through pumps and redwood wiers and steel screw-gate pipes, driving a pickup truck hundreds of miles each week on our own roads, hiring and firing the crew, deeply absorbed by my abstract responsibilities, rushing along our levee banks like a military man engaged in games of conquest.

We bought canned goods by the truckload. No one had time to bother with a garden. We were not so much interested in growing things as we were in power over nature. I came to hate the work and the valley I had so loved in the beginning. Eventually we sold out.

On spring mornings in Montana, when the runoff comes, I pull on knee-high rubber boots and walk out across the meadows behind the log house where my true love lives, to walk along splashing in the water. Birds call, clouds gather over the mountaintops beyond the Big Blackfoot River. I am surrounded by daisies and wild roses as I shovel up little dams in the sodded ditches, working the water along some ridge of high ground. It's another try at directing flow in the world, but this time, once again, it is play, as life mostly should be, I think. Sometimes I crouch, lost in the stink of growth, and watch the long-legged insects walk on the water, and imagine I am home again.

PART TWO

Lost Cowboys and Other Westerners

1

As a small boy I liked to get out of the house early and catch the yellow Adel school bus as it began its run on the gravel roads, picking up the children of neighbors. They were mostly Irish, a generation or two out of County Cork, girls in home-sewn clothing and boys with home-cut hair, but in important ways they were just like me. Their families were inventing a new life, like we were, and owned land and ran cattle. The men in all our families were cattlemen. That was what counted.

There was a girl who didn't have any father we knew, or any men at home. Her mother was the rancher, and she mostly kept company with horses and cattle, riding out alone into the Warner Mountains, haying her acres of meadow in the summer and feeding off a wagon in the winter.

Every morning the girl got on the bus and sat by the window, alone in our midst. She was a year or so older than I was, serious, taken to be gifted, mysteriously beautiful, and silent. There was a season or so, about the age of ten, when I thought I loved her. Then my father sent me to school in California, and fifty years got away.

A couple of summers ago I was back in the valley, touching at the past, and I saw her again, a lank woman with gray hair wrapped in a bun, her boots run over and her work pants out at the knees, picking up her mail at the Adel Store, silent and absolutely her. I want to think she knew me. "So this," she seemed to be saying, "is how it came out."

What I want this to be is an adding up of reasons for taking care, a calculation that would be a start at naming useful dreams, like the one in which I lay me down and run these sights through the eye of my thinking, and drift to sleep without once fearing the moment when all I am will vanish forever in the energies of what we are.

What I want are stories about animals like us, and fecundity, one seduction and then another until we are all satisfied with our lives in the make-believe.

On my list of dreams are huge straight-grained larch along evergreen hillslopes of the northern Rockies as they turn golden and shed their needles on October afternoons in the high country, needles filtering down like some kind of bright rain into the fishing streams, onto us as we walk, and springtime in the palm tree oasis in the Sonoran Desert, and the odor of drying alfalfa along with memories of gin drinking meditations at three o'clock in the starry darkness of mid-July in Warner Valley, in the high-desert distances of southeastern Oregon, which is still the main staging ground for my imagination. The stories are a thicket to catch the mind from falling.

Our urge to detail the intimate particularities of the world we lived in as a child is often, it seems, one of our ways of trying to return, to reconnect. If only we could be alive without the imagination standing between us and whatever is out there like some kind of movie scrim.

What would things look like if our minds would shut down with the imagining? What if we could stop ourselves from constantly participating in the invention, if we could quit making it up?

Would we then be as real as we were in the lost paradise that was childhood before the fall, before the world went away into make-believe? What about the idea that childhood is make-believe? We wonder where it went; we know it is all our fault. As if we had any choice.

We think we want to get out of ourselves, and escape, but there's no place to go except madness, which is impossible to talk about as a destination. Like sexual orgasm, the actualities of craziness have to be considered ineffable and thus impossible, I think, to describe—even to ourselves.

We are driven to the rituals of connection we find in music and dancing and food and storytelling and narcotics and fucking while the rain falls outside. I can hide my dis-ease under booze or hard labor or good works or literature, or any other obsession. But it comes back in the morning.

That's what I did for so long in the taverns, patch over the hole. But my cures were not cures at all; they were places to hide. Surrounded by people, I practiced irony and sarcasm, the easiest arts.

I thought there was no way to discriminate between things that are valuable and things that are not; I thought we didn't have any politics. But we did. There in those Montana taverns we were trying to practice the arts of communality and compassion.

Like anybody, we were enclosed in stories and often couldn't see out. We wanted various coherencies to stand as valuable in ultimate ways, worth any defense necessary. Our imaginations turned us toward love of the imagined (one another), generating empathy and compassion. Our politics turned out to be ultimately ecological.

The more vividly we stock our recollections with detail, the more deeply we become engaged in ordering that detail. We recall what we understand as actual, and our imaginations get involved in the creation. Our stories slide in the direction of make-believe. What we know is always partway fiction.

The world is part of the long invention that is our life, the most important character after ourselves, the coherent place we can name—it exists like a friend, somebody to know, somewhere to feel safe. But it cannot defend itself, and we are destroying it increment by increment at a horrific rate. We must understand that we'll never be able to buy it back. Think of a story in which we come to understand that the complexity of the living world cannot be replicated no matter how much science fiction we hear about cities in space. It would be a story in which it sinks in on everybody that this is the only place we will ever be able to live.

If we cherish, with proper selfishness, whichever dream we inhabit, we must honor our need to revere ourselves and each other. If we want to be happy at all, we might see that we have no choice but compassion.

But it's pointless to imagine we can wrap mythologies around us like garments. Old stories are like maps—follow far enough and we find ourselves off the edge, in free-fall. Clouded in dreams, what we have is also actual and must be treated as if it were inside our skins, which it is in a more than metaphoric sense.

So many of us are dread-filled, driven to repetitively act out certain stories in hopes the enactments might defend us, save us, protect us. Much of the time frightened and defensive, we occasionally act and react like schoolyard children.

Enclosed in stories we grew up believing, we often can't see out. We want to see coherencies we grew up with as valuable in absolute ways. We enshrine our defenses (fears) in societal rules that force us to inhabit a relentlessly confrontational culture (the military and capitalist economics, the court system). Our system of law from the Constitution down is primarily a way of institutionalizing the winner-take-all nature of our society.

In contrast, some Japanese revere a quality in poetry they call *aware*, which in its widest sense means acknowledging the natural poignancy that resides in the transient beauty of temporal things that are inexorably fated to disappear, exactly as evanescent as any story. They are willing to enjoy a thought like this: How did the glory of our foolish afternoon with the luminous children dissolve into nothing but memory?

They are willing to understand that we are mostly up to nothing much but feeding ourselves and our urge to know, enjoying what we take to be beauty, protecting ourselves and loving our home and kind, giving in to the understanding that there is, actually, nothing much more than that *to do*.

We are hunted and hunters. We relate to places in hunting terms, as predator and prey. The killer inside us wants to look down on the gaming fields from some place of advantage, a prospect, a mountaintop. And the poor hunted part of us yearns for a hideaway, a refuge. Such needs are built into our genes. We want to feel sheltered as we look out over the playground.

We say we are suffering from a wound, a fall from a place where we imagine the animals lying down with one another, where they are content to be part of one another. We want to think our condition is temporary, or pathological. We want to believe we can be healed.

We tell stories to talk out the trouble in our lives (otherwise so often unspeakable). It is our main way of turning our lives sensible. Trying to live without such stories can make us crazy. They help us at working toward recognitions, insights, truths— that's what stories are most seriously for; they help us find what we believe to be holy in the world, and to identify what we hold demonic.

My code of freedom was also a code of selfishness. I could imagine myself as aggressive and *enfranchised,* and that sort of released me, but it was only some of the time a good idea.

I worked hard, seven days a week, for years, and everybody knew it. I was decent as I could be to the men who worked for me. I was Chairman of the Adel school board. I was incessantly responsible. I never touched women other than my wife except once or twice. I was almost always sober. Those were the kinds of points I had; that was who I was.

In 1963 I started spending my points. I was afraid of being tricked by a world that can withhold its love. I built my defenses, I had taught myself to fear the world, I couldn't even love myself.

Edward Abbey told me to be careful about coming to the age of fifty. "The world wears out on you," he said. "Your stomach goes to hell."

It's true, your stomach does go to hell, if you have used it at all with booze and peppery food. And—worse—the new wears off. Life can become a series of repetitions, night after night. You think you have tasted everything, to the point where you can guess what is coming next. You think you know all the songs. Which, you know, is ridiculous.

You become someone who always orders a certain brand-name gin in the summertime, even when you know it is going to be mixed with fresh orange juice or diet tonic. You'll never taste the difference. You like the continuity. It helps you know who you are. You are the person who orders brand-name gin.

During a talk in Missoula Paul Fussell said, "Travel is largely a business of intentionally journeying into yourself and what you mean in relation to the rest of the world and all of history." Some of us yearn to return to the old simplicities and alertness of childhood, and *see* the world again, vividly, to listen and smell and finger the textures like natives as we imagine them, or like animals.

For some diverted moments each day I would inhabit elaborately imagined visions of fantasyland sexuality. The drive of such imagining inhabits our lives for a long time. As we age, it stays with us like a dimming sunset. We mourn the loss as it goes. Our sexual fantasies are dreams of freedom, among the most potent we have. Very old people say such notions come back on them strong in their age. It is a way of traveling into the world.

So, the question seems to be: Why in my family, and mostly in my part of society so far as I can tell, can't we learn to connect to one another, at least more of the time, in even the most simpleminded, hand-holding ways? Why couldn't we ever do so, in my family, in my country, or anywhere I ever was?

William Kittredge

In looking for answers I want to forgo the single-cause cautionary tale. I want my questions to reflect our aching and common confusions, the ways they reflect themselves in our ways of initiating and educating ourselves into our responsibilities.

Surely, if we knew what to want, we would tell our children. Or maybe not? For a long time I thought that I had been tricked by my own mother and father. I saw them going about their lives with what seemed such assurance, and I wondered why they never told me anything actually useful, ever, really?

I think of the strobe-light shadows I love to recall from the jazzy clubs of my youth, and the streaks of sundown light across the floors of old taverns with their doors standing open to summer, places I still adore. What I like in my memories of those jazzy places and what I still find useful in Missoula taverns is the way they encourage me to seize and settle on the pleasures of the day.

We sometimes confuse ourselves with dreams in which serious harm can never come. Watch out, angels whisper, paradise is an invention; it is actual energies that are sacred.

There is nothing more dangerous than some of us, some of the time, released and enfranchised. Voices can begin to make themselves heard, and urge us to heedless dreams of conquest and revenge.

The operative word is *heedless.* When we no longer find it in ourselves to heed any consequences we discover that we have always possessed power. The very aged, about to die, have such power, as do potential suicides when everyone knows about them, and killers heading down to the schoolyard. Once that first shot is fired, someone said, they don't give a shit if the sun comes up. *Get rid of everybody but us.* Dead children in some playground, or a day-care center in Oklahoma City.

Voices can tell us that our baby-brained anger and paranoia are justified. They are unlikely to prescribe the virtues of patience. You, they whisper, are the first person.

But such freedom can also release us to engage life, get sexy and fall into love with a place or a kind of light at a certain hour, or a bird or a person or some other ecology, a way of regarding the world in which we are awash with compassion for the beloved and a yearning to cherish and preserve and keep from harm. Such freedom is also at the heart of political possibility.

A lovely woman I know unexpectedly started complaining that she no longer could get herself downtown on Saturday night. She wanted to sweat and dance to the old rock and roll, and take home a stranger to fuck until daylight, when he would go properly back to his hippiness.

"Some girl has taken my place," she said, and she grinned. We were happy boys and girls in our dream of equality (the idea that sexuality and freedom are so intertwined is very Puritan someone told me; but maybe it is only natural). To love, someone said, becomes more urgent as we grow older and the world fills up with death. "Fucking around" is a once in a while livable ideal, often desired, occasionally actual, sometimes boring.

The specific world, thick and rich with the stink of blooming flowers and sex and dustiness, seems necessary to us because of our genes, psychic possibilities encoded into our DNA. Isolate us altogether and we are apt to go mad. Go long enough without being touched and you will come to exist almost entirely in visions. It's always happening in country music.

Everything that is interesting, Céline says, happens in the shadows; we know nothing of the real life of the human race. I think he is at least partway right. There seems to be a gap between so much of what we actually do and the things we are willing to even try talking or thinking about.

While it is commonplace to know that life can go pointless when we start mistaking our games for purposes, it is much more difficult to actually stay in touch with anything like real purposes in a culture so mirror-faced as ours. It's clear we are not much capable of thinking or talking about the hungers which actually drive us. Aimed in that direction, our language doesn't work so good, it's not so facile. So we find certain things frightening, and we put them from our minds because we can't find names for them. We talk about instincts and that doesn't explain anything.

In a small town not far from Missoula there's an elegant yellow nineteenth-century bungalow with white trim and beveled windows and a wide veranda porch. It stands in the shadows of cottonwood above a sod-banked creek. Clusters of red and blue helium-filled balloons were floating against the yellow-painted ceiling above the veranda porch, bobbing in a breath of air.

I imagine children on a trampoline. What kind of singularity on earth am I trying to invent? Is our happy land still partway intact? Our lilac bloom, and buzz with honeybees and hummingbirds. Can we find ways to live in some approximation of home-child heaven?

2

It is often said that something may survive of a person after his death, if that person was an artist and put a little of himself into his work. It is perhaps in the same way that a sort of cutting taken from one person and grafted onto the heart of another continues to carry on its existence even when the person from whom it has been detached has perished.

Marcel Proust, *Remembrance of Things Past*

The thing I believed in, in the beginning, was the stories. If they were not worth doing there was no justifying anything. Good writing, I thought, would be like a license to steal. Anything, I thought, was forgivable to people who were writing well. Which is a line of bullshit a lot of people have used to excuse endless selfishness, cruelty, and cheapshit misconduct.

This is what I have learned to think since then: No one thing justifies any other thing. Each thing you do stands alone, they don't add up, not in any direction; nothing accumulates; the work you do is the work you got done, good or bad, and it doesn't earn you any moral advantage. If you have the luck to do good work, that's a fine thing. But it has nothing to do with making you anything but lucky.

At Iowa I worked with Richard Yates. He taught responsibility. "I can't see the point," he said, talking about characters in stories, "in making a straw man, then lighting him afire to prove he'll burn." There was no point, Yates seemed to be saying, in implying life was less than it is. We are usually bewildered, and mostly capable of transcending ourselves.

In the summer of 1971, under the eye of the owner, Alfred Cipolato, we drifted along the narrow aisles of the Broadway Market in Missoula and bought tins of mussels fired in butter, mortadella, headcheese sausage and bottles of picked asparagus, a round of brie and Greek olives and bleu cheese and feta and four varieties of hard and harder salami, garlic pickles and Ameretti chocolates, Mumm's Cordon Rouge, a case of Orvieto, Pescevine wine in fish-shaped bottles, and expensive crackers. We bought at least that much.

Listings are attempts to make existence whole and holy in the naming. We were mounting an expedition to Flathead Lake, intricate shorelines around a huge expanse of trolling water, the natural look of things mostly intact, a place where anything goes, another weekend with motorboats.

I had brought my new wife to Montana from the lava-rock deserts of southeastern Oregon and a society that can be called ranch-land monoculture; we felt privileged to be in a place so populated and exotic as Missoula.

Mister Cipolato was telling us about reading poems by the

Italian poet Montale (Nobel Prize, 1975) to a class at the University of Montana taught by the poet Richard Hugo. "They needed to hear it in the real language," Cipolato said.

"'Ugo," he said, "does not understand Montale." This was it, our new world, literary gossip while our multilingual grocer sliced sweet Virginia ham for us to carry away in a little private paper sack.

When I first knew him, Dick Hugo lived in a scheme thick with spooks; ghosts of love. But he also lived in such a way as to make that seem perfectly normal; most of us, his poems seemed to say, were fated to failure, and memories of loss. *The Blue Angel* was his favorite movie.

In 1971 Dick scared himself sober for a number of years, and got his work done, work he owed himself after a lifetime of devotions. He had labored at learning to speak in a voice that was absolutely forgiving, and gave us the best of it as the booze wore off and he looked around to a world bright with significances.

Dick married a second time and was the man he meant to be —he traveled, then drifted back into drinking like he'd never been gone, which is the way with big-time alcoholics. Dick lost a lung to surgery, and a couple of years later died in a cancer ward, of pneumonia, almost at once after it was discovered he had leukemia.

Dick Hugo was my necessary friend. More than anyone he educated me, but I didn't want to know about the look of things in coffins. I almost managed to ignore his death.

But not quite. Maybe we don't know enough if we have never been cut to the bone, by which I mean quite literally cut, the elastic flesh drawing open from the blade. Deep within we catch a glimpse of the treasure, our own white bone. A voice was whispering: *Don't worry, you'll get your chance.* I tried to quit smoking.

Some years ago I was shambling along through the post-tennis crowds outside the Sun Valley Lodge with a half-dozen old friends. We were there for a conference called "The Writer and the West." Jesus, I thought, here I am, at last, safe in the significant world.

Not a half mile away, over the creek and up on a sage-covered hillslope, the stucco of Hemingway's last house flared deep pink in the late sun. At the age of thirty-four he started asking people to call him Papa. But we were bulletproof; we would never be lonely like him, driven so crazy.

When I quoted, a few pages back at the beginning of this section, a passage from Proust, it was another writer, Ray Carver, whom I had in mind. Which is no doubt a strange way to begin a story about traveling to visit Ray, who had just missed dying. Or, as it turned out, not escaped. In fact he was dying. But of course we all are. That was what I told myself.

In December 1987, just after Christmas, Annick Smith and I drove the freeways from Montana to visit my children and grandchildren and some friends in Seattle. We ate fresh oysters; we played with frivolity and cultivated the idea that it is possible to live without guilt amid the pleasures of paradise; we tried to ignore the idea that Ray was dying not so far away, at least I did, then Annick and I drove over to Port Angeles on the

Olympic Peninsula, where Tess Gallagher and Ray were seeing to what was the end of his life.

The rhododendrons were flowering, and the azaleas (or so it seems in memory), and Ray was fragile (a large, awkward man gone breakable) but not at all what you would think of as killed. Annick and I bought cut flowers in a shop on the main street in Port Angeles, and took them up through the incessant rain to Ray's big old-fashioned two-story house on the hill above the harbor; Ray made us some of his good coffee (he'd gone to coffee when he quit booze; it had become one of his specialties). We sat in the bright kitchen with the cut flowers on the drainboard, and drank the coffee, and pretty soon we were talking. It was raining outside and quiet and Ray told us his story about healing from the almost unimaginable operation, the removal of about two-thirds of one cancerous lung. He'd coughed up some blood one November morning in a kind of innocent, almost painless way, and the nightmare began. That was how he put it.

"It was a nightmare," Ray said. Sunlight broke through, casting long streaks of gunmetal brilliance across the seawater toward Vancouver Island. He smiled. "But now we're all right," he said. Something like that.

I was watching Ray like he was in possession of some secret message I could read if only I could pay close enough attention. The thought did not last but a second, a sort of easily forgettable twinge I put away as if such self-interest while face-on with the oncoming death of a friend were shameful. And maybe it is. The message I was looking for had something to do with taking care of yourself by cherishing what there was to cherish, moment into moment, and not holding to it—something like that, some secret Ray knew, and I didn't, some story he had learned.

For a while that evening Annick and I were alone in Ray's house, and I sat in the chair where Ray sat when he read; I held his books and opened them to the place where he had closed them. There was a good tape deck, and dozens of classical tapes. I played some Vivaldi, trying to fathom this man who had been my friend in another life, before he was dying, trying to hear what he heard, as he heard it. He was reading mostly European poets. Milosz, some others I can't remember. I'm moved to think of poetry I know closer to heart, Philip Levine:

> *Earth is eating trees, fence posts,*
> *Gutted cars, earth is calling her little ones,*
> . . . .
> *They lion grow.*

Ray was a man who had stared himself down in the mirror of his imagination, and now he was dying without allowing himself to descend into any rattled bitterness, so far as I could discern. I was trying to see how he got to where he was, I was trying to understand how it could be that he could absorb the terrifying joke of this perfect metaphysical injustice into his calmness and turn it reasonable, at least into something no more unnatural than the running water that drowns some mother's blessed child.

Ray and I had been friends since the spring of 1970, and we liked to tell ourselves, as he said in one of his stories, that we had *seen some things*. We met one spring evening in the old Olympic Hotel in Seattle, perfectly by accident, and we fell for one another as inebriates will, like playmates in love with the same possibilities.

There was some college comp-class English teacher's gathering in the Olympic. The lobby was given over to a vast display of books, a hundred or so yards of publisher's booths. But it was empty when I wandered through in the early evening.

Empty, that is, except for one scruffy fellow who was way down the line. As I was looking through a book called *Short Stories from the Literary Magazines* this fellow came right up to my elbow and tried to look over my shoulder. "I've got a story in there," he said.

"Yeah," I said. "I'll bet you do."

"Please be quiet please," he said.

I knew what he meant, but I didn't believe it.

"It is," he said. "It's mine. Curt Johnson put it in there. He printed it in a magazine called *December.*"

It was not a lie anyone would have bothered telling, at least in those days. It was clear this man was Raymond Carver, and I was one of the people in the world who would have found significance in that fact. This stranger had written the story called "Please Be Quiet, Please." It was already a kind of famous story in my mythologies.

A couple of years before, I had read that story in a hotel room in Portland, sitting with my feet up in the bed and disengaged from the world and waiting for my second wife to come back from somewhere, and that story got me started again in my wondering if I had already ruined my life. "Please Be Quiet, Please" caused me to hang my head with heartbreak over my own situation in the world and yet to admire myself for even trying to confront those troubles as a writer.

However stupid it sounds, that is pretty close to what I thought right after I read "Please be Quiet, Please" one rainy afternoon in the old Benson Hotel in Portland while I yearned to be actual at something. For a moment that story led me to think I was doing the right thing with my life.

And here I was, better yet, in another hotel, with the guy who wrote the story. This was indeed the life; we were shy for some moments, then we touched, we shook hands, we talked about a cup of coffee. Wait a minute, he said, why not a beer, I said why not a drink. A drink would be fine, maybe a couple of drinks, what the hell; all things lay before us. It was that moment between drunks that is known as Exchanging Credentials. Would you have a drink? Well, maybe, sure.

Even on the morning of this writing, a brilliant blue day that began with temperatures well below zero, after an evening of Christmas celebration with family, I think of the old days and going down to the taverns in Missoula to join the people I know. They are still there, some of them, and I still love the thought of their company. There was a time when we would be drunk by noon.

The days after Christmas, in the taverns, were always splendid in their timelessness. At heart loomed that perfect irresponsibility, long hours when it was possible to believe we were invisible and shatterproof, walking on water for at least a little while, and beautiful in our souls.

But those afternoons are gone. Ray took a hard fall on the booze. Drink became his secret companion in a more profound way than anything, even love, ever really works for most of us.

We pulled our tricks. It was our only sport; it would never

end; we were free, invulnerable. In June 1973, running on get-away bravado and whiskey, I took a long run from Missoula and found myself at Carver's house in Cupertino.

My first day in town we made our way over to a literary party in Berkeley, in some public room on the campus. I found myself talking to a famous critic with a glass of white wine in my hand, thinking in my drunken self-pretense that I knew some never-before-revealed thing about *texts*. Ray lifted a sack of ice over his head, crashed it down on the corner of a trestle table, and three half-gallons of gin danced off to shatter on the stone floor. We hired a graduate student to drive us back to Cupertino.

And we lived there in dreams for a week, drinking two bottles of vodka every day, one for each of us. In the morning I would come out of my bedroom to find Ray in the living room with vodka, orange juice, ice, my drink mixed.

Toward the end of the week we wandered up to the little liquor store at the high end of Cupertino Road, and ordered a half gallon. "Christ," the clerk said. "You guys together?"

Crossing the twilight of a moving-picture six-plex parking lot on the west side of San Jose, I looked back to see Mary Ann looking back another fifty yards to the place where Ray stood beside their little yellow Japanese automobile. He had waited until we moved off toward the theater and then come up with a pint from under the seat, and now he was downing the last of it, chin to the China pink of the evening sky and oblivious to us in what he thought of as his selfishness.

That fall Ray was teaching full time in Iowa City, in the Writers' Workshop with the likes of John Cheever, feeling that he was some semblance of the real thing since there he was with Cheever, who was damned sure the real thing and as much a drunk as anybody.

Every Friday afternoon Ray was supposed to meet a beginning poetry writing class at College V, UC Santa Cruz. It was possible; he could fly every Thursday afternoon, meet his class, and fly back to Iowa City in time to meet his workshop on Tuesday. He had worked a deal with one of the airlines. Free tickets in swap for an essay (which of course never got written) for some airline magazine.

No problem. Two jobs, two paychecks, home every weekend.

And he showed up on the airplane each Thursday evening for a number of weeks. Always drunk. I had left my second wife behind in Missoula and was thrashing around in the single life again, temporarily, according to my plans anyhow, at Stanford with a Stegner Fellowship. So I was available and I drove him down the fifty or so miles to Santa Cruz, and he ceremoniously pinned a notice to the door of his classroom: *Can't teach. Sick.* And it was true.

The next week Ray lay down in the backseat of my car so no one could possibly see him, and it was my job to pin up the notice. The week after that Chuck Kinder and I went down without Ray. The class was mostly hippies with no shoes. We faced a circle of their bare grass-stained feet propped up around our conference table. Kinder refused to look. I carried on like some prideful piss-ant. That was the last of those classes; Ray stopped coming altogether.

That Christmas there was a swaying in the warm winds; Ray flew to Missoula, then drove south with my second wife and Ed McClanahan, who was taking my place in Missoula. It sort of seemed like we all might couple up again and make peace and be lovey. And we kind of did, for a week or so.

Ray and Mary Ann looked to be bemused by happiness as they drifted off from a small party at McClanahan's house in Palo Alto. It wasn't until the next day that I got a full report. It was one of our sports in those days, getting the full report.

Ray had lost Mary Ann. I mean lost her. He got in the car and drove the twenty-some freeway miles from McClanahan's to his place in Cupertino, innocently, without Mary Ann. Ray left her standing at the curb, door locked on her side. Rather than come back into McClanahan's, Mary Ann hitched a ride with an old couple. There was lots of hitching rides in those days; people fell out, temporarily. The old couple drove Mary Ann right to her door. Ray was rummaging in the refrigerator. "Oh," he said, when Mary Ann came in the door. "I wondered where you were."

At least that was how it was reported. Ray said he was slicing a sweet onion, a Walla Walla sweet, for a huge thick sandwich. Later on he never ate. That was one way you told the beginning of the end; some people stopped eating.

Maybe Ray was the more easily wounded, maybe he was physically fragile, or maybe he was simply capable of taking all of what was happening more seriously than most of us, maybe he saw through our joke in a clearer way, maybe he was more open to certain kinds of wounding, to witnessing what became our war zone with a heart not so securely boarded up and barricaded as, at the least, was mine.

Maybe Ray recognized that in the long run we weren't reaping freedom after all; we had been tricked.

I hope there is not anything about this recital of antics that sounds prideful, like the kind of stories you dine out on. Once there was, once I used them that way. At least I recall telling them in bars while we all had a swell time; they had a certain currency.

Ray suffered some sight of chaos deep in his soul and turned away and sobered up in the middle 1970s, and moved up to McKinleyville on the coast of California just north of the little university town of Arcata, where he had gone to school in the old days, and where friends like Dick Day could help see him through the drying out. I visited there a couple of times, on my way to San Francisco. I asked Ray if he was writing. By this time he had been sober for most of a year. "No," he said. "I could. But I'm not."

I asked him why.

"Because I can't convince myself it's worth doing."

That time he surprised me. I thought about that for days afterwards. It implied a kind of consequence I had never anticipated. We had seen a lot of our things by then, but it had never seemed to me possible that even the fractured marriages and falling-down, bite-your-tongue convulsions in the streets could lead to this kind of seriousness. Ray must have witnessed some things I had not imagined.

A lot of the long-term Sunday afternoon sadness in taverns where I go, among people I know, has to do with wasted possibilities, fine and capable people who didn't do any work, and collapsed into serving their own selves and pleasures, as I was so inclined to do, for so long. Drunk in the morning. Those were fine times, I have to say, with fine friends. I loved them dearly.

But it has been a good idea, for me, to attempt putting away the indulgence and make-believe, and try to identify some decencies to serve. I do not mean god or country, but community, which is a larger, extended version of our own selves. We are responsible; nothing is bulletproof.

These were not thoughts I let myself dwell on in those days. Most of what I did was support a set of all-day excuses for seldom doing any work. Maybe Ray has seen some visions, I said to myself, maybe that was his deal. Maybe the heebie-jeebies had scared him. I was not scared.

And there we were, not so many years later. He was famous, and dying. I began to think about what I knew of Ray's life as a teaching story; I began thinking about learning from his willingness to deal with what was actual. I was studying him for hints.

In the months before his affliction revealed itself Ray had taken to inspecting condominiums on the downtown hills of Seattle overlooking Elliot Bay and shipping lanes to the Orient, right near the Public Market with its perfect produce and living geoducks you could kill and fry for dinner, and flowers picked just that morning. He liked to talk about living close to such amenities.

Just out the windows you could witness sunset over the Olympic Mountains. This was the saw-filer's son from Yakima, and he was finally getting his chance at the world. He wanted properties.

A few years before, in the fall of 1982, while I was visiting in southern Vermont, Ray showed up driving an immaculate new Mercedes. He had been going home to Syracuse from John Gardner's funeral, he said, and he had decided you might as well enjoy some things, if you could afford them. "So what the hell," he said. "So I bought this car. Who knows?"

And that was what we were all studying, on that visit to Port Angeles, "Who knows?"

What I was most concerned about, that last time there, was watching myself as I watched Ray and wondered who to be, studying him like a stranger, envying his equilibrium. He had survived some series of transformations, and I wanted to share the wisdom, if it was wisdom. Ray was dying and I wanted to know how he could conduct himself as he did, I wanted to see what he saw when he looked out from his seashore to the flow of his ocean. I wanted to hear his music as he heard it.

The summer before, I had gone to Port Angeles for some salmon fishing. It all seemed so very easy, that dream, and natural enough. We caught salmon, the day was brilliant, Ray was the generous center of it all, our prince of good fortune, proof that some rewards were justly rationed out by the way of things. And now his life was over, soon now, forever. Someone had canceled his ticket to the rest of the party.

On a bright chill morning, Ray and Tess and Annick and I took a short hike on a downhill path to the edges of the beach, where we were stopped by driftwood logs. Ray was still healing from his operation and moving like an old man. He refused to climb over the logs, and we turned inland along the soggy fairways of a little golf course bordering a tiny creek and looped back to a bridge over the river. It was a small expedition into the native world, but it took longer than ever before. Back at Tess's house, Ray opened a tin of canned salmon, we ate a little, and that is what there is to tell. There is no insight here, no moment, no recognition.

There is just my friend in his gentle patience with his terrible fate, and with us.

He could have been impatient; he could have thought we were exhausting what little remained of his life. And maybe he did. Or maybe he was glad of the company.

On August 3, 1988, in warm morning sunlight on a patio outside a mental health clinic in Aspen, Colorado, I was meeting with a fiction-writing class. "I see in the paper," one of them said, "where your friend is dead." He was talking about the New York *Times*. Ray was dead at fifty, leaving the example of his conduct while dying.

In December 1988, coming home from the beaches near La Push, Annick and I passed by a chaos of clear-cut logging near the little town of Forks — heedless wreckage, mile-long swatches of torn earth and the jagged rotting stumpage of the cedar trees, limbs crushed into the black mud. Imagine the earth perfectly violated.

We stopped in Port Angeles and visited the seacoast highland where Ray is buried. Tess had worn a little path around the grave. She went down there and talked to him, she said. I tell him the news, she said. Like all of us, Ray was given to a love of gossip and scandal. His eyes would gleam, and he would lean into the talk. But as I stood there by his grave I had nothing much in the way of things to say to the dead, except to make a game of my question. How is it, old sport?

Maybe I was too scared for much fun.

> I said to myself: how many happy, contented people there really are! What an overwhelming force they are! Look at life: the insolence and idleness of the strong, the ignorance and

where, overcrowding, degeneration, drunken-
ness, hypocrisy, lying— Yet in all the houses
and on all the streets there is peace and quiet;
of the fifty thousand people who live in our
town there is not one who would cry out, who
would vent his indignation aloud. We see the
people who go to market, eat by day, sleep by
night, who babble nonsense, marry, grow old,
good-naturedly drag their dead to the ceme-
tery, but we do not see those who suffer and
what is terrible in life goes on everywhere behind the scenes. Everything is peaceful and
quiet and only mute statistics protest: so many
gallons of vodka drunk, so many children dead
from malnutrition— And such a state of things
is evidently necessary; obviously the happy
man is at ease only because the unhappy ones
bear their burdens in silence, and if there were
not this silence, happiness would be impossible.
It is a general hypnosis. Behind the door of
every contented, happy man there ought to be
someone standing with a little hammer and
continually reminding him with a knock that
there are unhappy people, that however happy
he may be, life will sooner or later show him its
claws, and trouble will come to him—illness,
poverty, losses, and then no one will see or hear
him, just as now he neither sees nor hears others. But there is no man with a hammer. The
happy man lives at his ease, faintly fluttered by

small daily cares, like an aspen in the wind, and
all is well.

Anton Chekhov, *"Gooseberries"*

Chekhov understood that stories, when they are most valuable,
are utterly open in their willingness to make metaphor from
our personal difficulties. Our most useful stories focus simulta-
neously on our most generous and betraying ways. These troubles could be yours, the story says, this unfairness *is* yours, and
so are these glories.

Ray must have spent lots of time listening to Chekhov's
person with the little hammer. It is easy to see that his most
profound sympathies lay with the disenfranchised, the saw-
filers like his father, as did Chekhov's.

Ray's last story, "The Errand," is about the death of Chekhov, drinking champagne as you die, celebrating what there is
to celebrate, which is this, what we have. It is one of his put-
yourself-in-my-shoes, try-my-blindness stories, like the story
in which a man stands before a mirror in his neighbor's bedroom in his neighbor's wife's lingerie, making a try at being
someone else.

Ray gave the world all the strength and decency he could
muster and died out of an unnaturally foreshortened life (as we
do; each of us). By his time of dying Ray had come to what
seemed a learned and objectified sense of his own beliefs; he
found it to say, sure enough, sadness all over town—but, like
my man Chekhov, I'm going to forgive myself, and try happiness anyway.

However terrifyingly misguided our lives may have been,
we have to pray they are ultimately forgivable. My culture has

poured burning napalm on babies; the people responsible did it on purpose; I didn't think I had any politics; much of what we do is madness.

We know the story of civilization; it can be understood as a history of conquest, law-bringing and violence. We need a new story, in which we learn to value intimacy. Somebody should give us a history of compassion, which would become a history of forgiveness and care-taking.

Ray's best work continually suggests the need for attempting to keep decent toward one another while we are deep in our own consternations. They are masterworks of usefulness; they lead us to imagine what it is like to be another person, which is the way we learn compassion. It is the great thing: In intimacy we learn to cherish each other, through continual acts of the imagination. Nothing could be more political. More of what we need in the West today.

3

During my year at Stanford University, I was a long time past the age when I should have been a "fellow" anywhere, and furiously driven to prove my own value. It was time to turn myself into a real writer. Some of my friends, Chuck Kinder and Jim Crumley and Max Crawford, were publishing novels, and Ray was already coming to national attention.

It was time to write something that would justify all the expense of spirit that had gone into refashioning my life. My first decade out of college and the Air Force, back on the ranch in southeastern Oregon, daydreaming about the day when I would be a writer, I fed off examples like Wallace Stegner, a boy out of the rural West who had gone on to have an important career. Driven crazy by those fantasies, I managed to lose my wife and children and the life I'd known since childhood. There I was, with a fellowship in Stegner's name, a stranger in paradise (California).

It was time to get down on some splendid novel in which all my ambitions would be realized. What I wanted was a terrific world-turning story. That's where the trouble started, with that killer ambition. It turned out I didn't know any world-turning stories. I didn't even have a story I understood as my own.

What I had were the strong feelings that had driven me to write in the first place—essentially my love of the things I had given up to be a writer. What I didn't have was any politics (which I think of as a way of understanding why one thing is more important than another). What I had was ambition. I would not have recognized an important story if one got into bed with me.

So I tried to make one up, whole cloth, about betrayal, which surely should have been one of my topics. Only I thought I was the person betrayed. My story wasn't grounded in anything close to emotionally actual—it was all froth and style.

But I worked hard; I had to, my life was at stake. I tried to patch over the holes in my story with high-gear prose, and Chuck Kinder said it read like page after page of science fiction titles. I stayed with it after I went back to Missoula. I had found a sure way of defeating myself, convincing myself that I would never be a writer of any consequence.

Which is where I was in the summer of 1976, defeated and drinking the days away in Missoula taverns, savoring a sense of doom, when Jim Crumley and Steve Krauzer and I drifted down to Sun Valley for a conference on Western movies. What I was looking for was a run of famous parties, and that's what I found. But I also found serious people talking about the prime mythology of my homeland. The Western, I came to understand, is a story about overweening ambition, and conquest. I went home with a start at a set of values (a way of seeing), and a topic—the necessity of empathy and compassion—without which ambition is pointless and some of the time deadly. I was on my way toward being able to name my story, which is to say, my work.

Years later, I was driving south across Nevada on Highway 95. There, through the steely afternoon distances, you get the sense that you are in a country where nobody will cut you any slack at all. You are in a version of the American West where you are on your own; the local motto is *take care of your own damned self*. I was just south of Tonapah, maybe a hundred and fifty miles north of Las Vegas, dialing across the radio, when I heard the news that Louis L'Amour was dead of lung cancer at the age of eighty.

They said he had published 101 books. The first was *Hondo*, in 1953, which was made into a movie starring John Wayne. It seemed right. The way I saw L'Amour, in the eye of my mind, he even looked like John Wayne. Remember that old man, perishing of cancer in *The Shootist*?

If you had never lived in the American West, you might have felt elegiac, and you might have imagined the last of the old legendary Westerners were dying. I knew better. Having grown up on a horseback cattle ranch, I knew a lot of those old hard-eyed bastards. They're not dying out. What was passing was another round of make-believe.

The old true Westerners I knew never had the time of day for shoot-out movies, and they mostly thought Western novels were just so much nonsense. They would soon tell you that much of what passes as authenticity in the Western, no matter how colorful and indigenous it might seem, was all at least ten percent wrong and must have come from library research. I remember my grandfather's scorn for a pulp paper copy of *Ranch Romances* he found in the bunkhouse when I was a kid.

"Book people," my grandfather said. "Nobody ever lived like that."

Driving Nevada, I felt a kind of two-hearted sadness over the death of Louis L'Amour. He so clearly loved the West and the dreams of the good strong people he found there, and yet he so deeply transmogrified any sense of the real life there that my grandfather might have understood and respected.

Most of us understand that the West we find in a Louis L'Amour novel didn't really exist much of anywhere. A lot of any art is trumped-up. We excuse it. Out in the Armagosa Valley of southern Nevada, just west of where I was traveling on Highway 95, there are great dunes of yellow sand, which have stood in for Africa and Arabia through all the history of movies. You don't hear much complaining about that kind of artifice.

There's a darker problem with the Western. It's a story inhabited by a mythology about power and the social utility of violence, an American version of an ancient dream of warrior righteousness. Because of that, it's a story many of us find threatening. We don't want to live in a society fascinated by fantasies of killer wish-fulfillment. We keep hoping the Western will just go away. But it won't. From *The Song of Roland* to *Shane* to *Star Wars*, these hero stories just duck out of sight, like Clark Kent stepping into a telephone booth, and reemerge with renewed vitality.

The dreaming goes on. We all know how Westerns proceed. There is the society of good simple folk who only want to live decent lives, and there are the evil unshaven bad guys, driven by undisciplined lusts and greed. And there is the hero, who cuts through the shit. Shane straps on his sixguns and solves the problem of Jack Palance. The obvious implications, taken seriously by a society like ours, so deeply and often frustrated, and so adept in the sciences of destruction, are literally unthinkable. Nuke the bastards.

After the Lone Ranger we get Dirty Harry and Rambo. In times many of us understand as awash in moral disorder, mostly because our problems are so complex as to defy clean quick-fix solutions, we yearn for simplicities, and it's natural enough some of us might dream of escaping into an imagined gunfighter past, and yearn to clear the decks. Enough with ambiguities.

So, when people told me the death of Louis L'Amour meant we were finally done with such stories, I had to say I didn't think so. Not at all. Louis L'Amour wrote books about a world in which moral problems were clearly defined, and strong men stepped forward to solve them. Which, in a complex world, is often a damned poor way of solving problems. Witness the bombing in Oklahoma City, or the killings at Ruby Ridge. But millions of people seem to have found that old hero story a very comfortable dream to inhabit. In some form, it's going to be with us a long time. And there's nothing so terrible about that; it's just that we have to keep from forgetting it's a fantasy and always was.

The thing I most strongly dislike about the Western is personal and has much to do with my love of the kind of country where I have always lived. What I resent is the way the Western has deluded so many of us in the West for so long.

The Western told us that we were living the right lives, and that we would be rewarded if only we would persevere. That message was a clear simple-minded lie. Driving Nevada, thinking about the death of Louis L'Amour and the shells of burnt-out hotels in one-time mining towns like Goldfield and Rhyolite, I felt anger ringing in me like the empty buzzing of locusts.

The dim shadows of leafy poplar far off against the mountains, with Death Valley beyond, were sure signs of pump agriculture. Right over there people were exhausting aquifers that had taken millennia to accumulate. And what energy there was in the little roadside clusterings of bars and cafes and brothels that comprise towns like Lathrop Wells and Indian Springs, along the highway on the western fringe of the Nuclear Testing Site, seemed trumped-up and painted on.

That roadside West is like a shabby imitation of our cowboy dreams, a sad compromised place, used and abused, and used again. So many of the people there feel deceived, and with good reason. They believed in promises implicit in the Western, that they had a right to a good life in this place, and it has become clear to them that it was all a major lie. *Take care of your own damned self.* Nobody is bulletproof.

What we need in our West is another kind of story, in which we can see ourselves for what we mostly are, decent people striving to form and continually reform a just society in which we can find some continuity, taking care in the midst of useful and significant lives. We're finding such storytelling, slowly, in books like *Housekeeping* and *A River Runs through It*, in the stories and essays and novels of writers like Mary Clearman Blew and Terry Tempest Williams and James Welch and Ivan Doig, Cormac McCarthy and Louise Erdrich and Leslie Silko and James Galvin and so many others. It's part of my two-hearted sadness that Louis L'Amour couldn't have come to appreciate the flowering of a genuine literature in the West he so loved.

I'm attempting to talk about the kinds of stories we live by and love out in the blue distances of America, which so often fail us anyway. In the West we draw strangers who seem to imagine they are gunfighters (maybe they come to us because they've read too much Louis L'Amour). We encounter them everywhere.

Back in 1970, I spent an evening at anchor out on Flathead Lake in a spacious old hardwood speedboat. Snowfields on the alpine peaks of the Mission Range were luminous orange in the evening light. We were watching osprey fall to the black water like stones as they fished for kokanee salmon, which they took to their young in their huge willow-stick nests on the tiny oriental-looking Bird Islands.

Except for the yellow-haired stranger wearing mirror-tinted glasses and a gold Rolex (he was rumored to be CIA, back from Asia and looking for a home; they were thick around town in those days) my companions were local and well-off; they owned timber, a ski resort. I said something about DDT, and the way it accumulates in the food chain, and what a sadness it was that the osprey were dying out (as they were at that time; contaminated by DDT, they were laying soft-shelled eggs). The stranger took off his dark glasses. His eyes were pale blue. "Fuck birds," he said. That man must have dreamed he was born to be merciless. He was inhabiting a silly story, and what he was, in a squint-eyed way, was a posturing fool.

We like to think America is a place where you can have a shot at being what you want to be; you can come to terms with yourself. Freedom, in a livable community, is supposed to be the point of things. It's our prime mythology, and it sort of works out, moreso if you're white and have some money. It's a story I try to live out; it doesn't have to fail. I walk down to the bars on Higgens Avenue in Missoula; I see people I never see anywhere else; some have been dead for a decade and I miss them.

We drove south through the ranchlands with Hart Mountain looming above us, stopping at the store in Plush for some talk. Many of the settlers around Plush are Irish from County Cork, and they brought a gift of vivid language from the old country. I recall a very old man and a very old woman, years ago, at a wake. The old man presented the old woman with a triple shot of Irish whiskey. "I don't think," she said, "I'll be drinking it."

"You'll be drinking it," he said, "or you'll be wearing it." So she drank it, and studied the floor and smacked her lips afterward while the old man smiled.

Winter days in Montana, snow blowing down the street, once you give up and decide they are going to last forever, are perfect for going to the barber shop. I was in the chair, the barber snipping around my ears, when a legendary entrepreneur, a man who had retired from the construction business with a clear fortune, came stomping through the door. He was cold, blowing on his hands, visibly excited.

After some small talk, he dug two Alka Seltzer bottles out of his topcoat pocket, held them to the light, and shook them. "Pure gold," he said.

He unscrewed the tops. The vials were filled with gold. I was jealous; this was power, the real thing, dug up and bottled, and he was showing it around in the barber shop; it's one of our customs, reverence for having, owning.

We are, most of us, ethnologists in our own house, working to locate ourselves amid the clutter. Some of us are quite self-consciously working to remake ourselves in the image of an imaginary long-ago land where people were healed to their lives.

But you have to think people have always been aware of their awareness and incessantly trying to avoid acknowledging how much everything, including ourselves, is on-the-spot in-vention and make-believe.

When I came to Montana I was always tracking but I didn't know what animal I was after. I would drift through the taverns like an anthropologist; I believed my life and the lives of people I knew were not of much significance because we lived in the insulated city of our middle-class affiliations. Lives of conse-quence, I thought, were being lived down the road among the drunks and Indians and working stiffs (as in, "Their lives are more *real*"; it was as condescending as could be).

Like a lot of people I imagined life in its most significant ca-dences was taking place somewhere on our political peripheries. I was after that occasional tavern that becomes a hide-out for radical funniness and the juxtaposition of unalike elements. A life in taverns can be like art, I thought, it can help us see freshly, our sacred duty.

Humiliation, and sentimental nostalgia, were dominant in

the cowhand music I listened to as the days drifted away. But I wasn't responsible; I was invisible and artistic, and close to paralyzed by my disengagements.

Can we learn to care about stories centered on gifts rather than getting, on giving away and learning to practice the arts of empathy? Maybe so. I'm reminded of an autumn afternoon in an enclosed area beside the West Fork of the Boulder River, where Laurie and Tom McGuane were putting their cutting horses through a light afternoon of work and exercise.

We'd had lunch on salmon Tom caught in Labrador; the horses were athletic and disciplined, beautiful; they must love what they do; they respond to touches and hints. The mountains in the Absaroka-Beartooth Wilderness were fringed with snow. It was all a little stunning, sort of perfect; I was a tiny bit jealous of Tom McGuane.

Tom had got himself a paradise my father would have loved, elegant pasturelands, intelligent horses, mule deer mating in the willows and wilderness just beyond, a tight traditional log house, prosperity, family; Laurie and her horse, Lucky Bottom '79, maybe the most articulate cutting horse ever to come out of Montana, danced in precise response to the cattle, and Tom said a thing I admired to the point where I wasn't jealous anymore. He said he loved the horses because they led him to see a little as they saw; Tom McGuane, more than many, lives within a set of fine privileges, some of which come to him because he is capable of moving beyond our usual preoccupation with self, to empathy and the natural consequence of empathy, compassion.

4

First you find a metaphor like the "lost wax process" in bronze casting (the idea of a residual metallic shell around a core that has melted and drained away—like cowboys in image instead of actuality), and then you name your manifestation of that metaphor (something like "Lost Cowboys"). You construct your piece of writing to fit the name. It's one way of trying to make sure your piece is reasonably coherent, and that it has a title you can live with.

There are at least four great memoirs about life on the plains, *Goodby to a River* by John Graves, *Old Jules* by Mari Sandoz, *Wolf Willow* by Wallace Stegner, and *We Pointed Them North* by Teddy Blue Abbott and Helena Huntington Smith.

The last time Teddy Blue ever saw Calamity Jane was in Gilt Edge, Montana, just up from the Judith Basin. "I joked to her about her trip and asked her: 'How'd you like it when they sent you east to get reformed and civilized?'

"Her eyes filled with tears. She said: 'Blue, why don't the sons of bitches leave me alone and let me go to hell my own route?' "

When Teddy Blue talked, it was always cowboying. The

later stuff was only life. "I started young and I am seventy-eight. Only a few of us are left now, and they are scattered from Texas to Canada."

"Such is life," Teddy said, "in the Far West."

Sliced apples and pears, various cheeses, decent wine: As evening came down over the tree-lined boulevards on the north side of Great Falls, there was a well-lighted reception in the Charlie Russell Museum.

A raggedy man came in off the street, boots wrapped with duct tape. Somebody told him the feast was free. He smiled and poured for himself.

Somebody wanted to show him out, but nobody did. What I remember is his judicious expression as he sipped his wine and studied a Russell painting, and the uneasiness in that hall full of the enfranchised (we the people with OK automobiles and new shirts).

The tension softened after somebody said the old man was probably the only person in the place Charlie Russell might have tolerated. Everybody smiled and knew it was true.

On summer evenings the year I turned six my father would catch a bay gelding called Moon, lift me to the saddle, and lead me out along the irrigation ditch at the head of the garden, where he would instruct me in the arts of horseback. If I came unseated, he would knock the dust off my shirt, and lift me up again; crying was unthinkable; this was my start in real life, and I knew it.

I remember daybreak on the high deserts of eastern Oregon, and my father and some other men who are dead now.

They would ease into a round willow-walled corral where sixty or so spooky geldings were circling counterclockwise around the rock-solid juniper center post. The cowboss threw his sea-grass *riata* in an effortless overhanded way and dropped a loop on a stocking-footed bay, and I watched as my father eased down the taut rope toward the trembling animal.

You see men like him in the Salt Lake City airport, surrounded by businessmen wearing polished snake-hide boots and skiers bound for the mountaintops with peacock feathers tucked into their hatbands. Not long ago I saw Wilfred Brimley in the Delta concourse at the Salt Lake City Airport, backed against a wall, studying the crowd (there, I thought, the first time I saw him on a movie screen, so actual amid the silliness of *The Electric Cowboy*, they got one of the real ones).

Another lank old broke-up buckaroo made his way past, limping and walking a little sideways like a crab, paying us none of his attention. It's my illusion that those old farts learned their rules in a rigorous school not many of us try any more (get back on your horse). They know their time is over, and hate it, as anybody would, as my father did; they see us as imitation and pitiful in our dislocations. Wilfred Brimley has become a movie star. I think of him as the first Old Postmodern Cowhand Fart, trapped in our zoo, keeper and kept. I wish I knew what he thought.

My father believed his second wife was as good and capable as a human could be, and yet he was willing to say no woman should ever be elected to political office. "They're not fit for it," he would say.

He despised the unemployed on principle, because they

were weak, but he was legendary for his generosity, and men who worked for him stayed for years. He loaned them money, bought them whiskey, hired them back, but he never imagined they were his equals. The list of things my father came to despise started and ended somewhere in the neighborhood of people who overwork the goodwill of others.

Snow was skittering across the highway at Lost Trail Pass in early November. I was backtracking Lewis and Clark south across the Bitterroot Mountains between Montana and Idaho. What I was seeking, in my lonely-boy state of mind, with Elvis plugged into the tape deck, was cure for my dislocations, and another growing season.

It's a dis-ease that can overcome you with first evidence of winter in the northern Rockies, when the world seems entirely distant from hummingbirds in the blooming lilacs. I'm growing old and people I know are dying of major afflictions; we're learning to accommodate the notion that closure, as in story and endings, has something to do with the people we are.

It was coming evening as I drove upstream along the Salmon River, out of isolated meadowlands along the great watersheds and into the deep forested canyons that rise toward the Stanley Basin. It's a drive everybody in Montana seems to try once in a while, seeking relief from our cherished isolations and heading south toward what we understand as heedlessness in Sun Valley, or gambling in Jackpot and Reno and then on to the alien blooming richness of the Sonoran deserts in early spring.

A few years ago my friend John Rember told me that he was finding dead, spawned-out salmon on gravel bars along the Salmon River. Not enough of them, yet, to raise the old-time rotting stench, but the big fish. He liked to think they might come back, thanks to the Sawtooth Fish Hatchery. Hatchery fish beat the hell out of the alternative, which was no salmon at all.

But I want more, and I grieve for the sad old terrible grizzly bears. The grizzlies in this part of the world were easy to kill. There was no need to go search them out in the bushwhack mountains. A hunter could just sight in his high-velocity rifle and wait for the salmon to run. The grizzly would come down to fish, and you could sit three hundred yards away with a scope, and kill them like pests. I pray that deep in these mountains there are grizzlies living invulnerable lives in a paradise of their own discovering, where we will never go.

In Stanley the white-water rafting tycoons had gone back to wherever they originate, and the village was settled in to enjoy a long season of rural privacy. John Rember is a native who left the family ranch south of Stanley in the late 1960s, graduated from Harvard, and learned to live in the land of the rich while he taught in a private school in Ketchum, where he climbed in the Sawtooths, and skied, season by season. He has cashed out to come home. When I visited he was living with his folks while he built a house of his own.

The locals are returning to roots. I did the other thing, left the valley where I grew up and never went back except to drive through on my way to somewhere else.

John and I walked the rough flooring in his new house. Out a hole in a wall, to be his bedroom window, in wintertime moonlight, the icy Sawtooth Range was glowing under a creamy, swirling sky, and I contemplated the classical, serious, fool-making mysteries. How to proceed? Can it be true we suffer a nostalgia for which there is no remedy on earth?

My nerves were wrecked. I imagined the morning light was breaking through the great windows in the Sun Valley Lodge like shattered glass. It should have been the sweetest of times, mayflies hovering in golden light under shimmering birch, the waters mysterious with eveningtime trout, and nights of ease and merriment among the winsome and perfectly enfranchised folk who inhabit the Wood River Valley.

I bribed the chambermaid for a peek into the third-floor bedroom where Hemingway is reputed to have written *For Whom the Bell Tolls*. It overlooked a year-round ice rink famous from 1930s Sonja Henie Ice Capades movies. What I found was intimacy with the kind of fracturing that drove Hemingway to his shotgun. Many must have it. I stood on the balcony, listening to birds. Their calling sang of dislocations.

So I eased myself downstairs. This was the summer of 1976. A Western Film Conference was underway: actors, old-time directors, scholars, stars, Harry Dean Stanton, Struther Martin, Buster Crabbe. I was there to learn something about the dominant mythology of my homeland.

That afternoon there were only a half-dozen meditative souls in the bar. I found myself in conversation with a couple of legendary men, the Native American actor Iron Eyes Cody and Colonel Tim McCoy of the Wyoming National Guard and MGM. As youngsters they had both gone to Hollywood from the Thermopolis country in Wyoming. They were bemoaning modernist inauthenticity, as old men will.

Don't mistake me, I respected them. Tim McCoy was one of the seven great stars at MGM before the invention of sound, him and John Gilbert, Lon Chaney, Ramon Navarro, Buster Keaton, Marion Davies, and Lillian Gish. It was perfect, there we were, remnants, me and those once-upon-a-time moving picture stars.

Then a green-eyed handsome man moved in. He was wearing an orange jogging outfit, deck shoes, no socks, and a Rolex watch. He eyed us like a hired pathologist. "What you need," he said to me, "is a line."

As in, we all thought, and we were right, cocaine.

As in, I think now, politics, line of work, and intention.

Colonel Tim McCoy just froze. Iron Eyes Cody looked away in sorrow. But it was true, I needed to be tethered. Many must have it. I smiled, and there I was, in complicity with the green-eyed guy, cut off from those old men and what I see to have been a chance at right relationship and true reverence. But the cocaine was also a try at connection. Which we are all after.

In Ketchum, over breakfast, a friend told about traveling to Santa Barbara four days a month to train as a lay analyst. Our talk led to notions of *familia*, the Latin word that unites home and family in a cluster of narratives, our most inclusive name for who we are.

We are all "making story." It is the most important thing we do. We constantly tell ourselves the story that is our life; when we forget the plot, we lose track of ourselves. We invent fine, brave, but sometimes wrongheaded stories to live by, and people to be. These can be teaching stories, good and useful, about learning to always seek humility and compassion. But the people inventing these stories, any of us, are wounded and frightened by the loneliness inherent in our lives, and our stories are often deeply selfish.

Many of us are heading out to the hills. To hell with public responsibilities. Maybe, we whisper, we can find a hide-out, water from a hot spring showering down from a cliff above a wilderness river. We are also talking about nature as a true resort, a place where we might find refuge. We are talking about privilege.

". . . the road took us to the most distant fountain of waters of the mighty Missouri in surch of which we had spent so many toilsome days and wristless nights."

—Meriwether Lewis

On a motel room TV I saw Elvis singing "You Ain't Nothing but a Hound Dog" to a real dog on the Steve Allen show in 1956. Meditating on Elvis's last sad rewards got me to Meriwether Lewis, and the high hopes that surrounded our beginnings.

On Monday, August 12, 1805, Lewis was laboring uphill, heading west toward the Continental Divide. Earlier in the afternoon a man named McNeal ". . . exhultingly stood with a foot on each side of this little rivulet and thanked his god that he had lived to bestride the mighty & heretofore deemed endless Missouri."

Lewis ". . . proceeded to the top of the dividing ridge from which I discovered immence ranges of high mountains still to the West of us with their tops partially covered with snow."

It was an instant of vast importance. The Corps of Discovery had been moving upriver from St. Louis for two days short of fifteen months, since May 14, 1804. One of the objectives assigned by President Jefferson was the discovery of an overland route for transcontinental trade and traffic. At last men from the United States were at the great watershed.

Lewis was expecting to gaze down on the River Columbia, a free-flowing highway that would carry them to the Pacific in triumph and ease. What he saw was timbered ridge after ridge, some snow-covered, feathering off to a sky that must have seemed more infinite with possibility than anyone had hoped.

Lewis and Clark returned to the East, and told Jefferson that the way to the West lay over a three-hundred-mile maze of mountains, sixty of which were covered with perpetual snows. Their message was taken to heart. The federal government did not venture into the Northern Rockies again until the Stevens railroad survey of 1855. An endlessness of mountains was left as an enclave to be inhabited by Indians, trappers, and prospectors, bypassed by civilization and civic order. Part of that enclave remains as wilderness in the intermountain West. It is vitally important to our sense of ourselves as a people, central in the story we tell about our national willingness to preserve what is most natural in our lives, if only by accident.

The entire West may be thought of as states on the cusp. If political boundaries had been laid out by a sensible formula, entities like Montana and Wyoming and Idaho wouldn't exist at all.

Almost a hundred years ago, in his *Report on the Lands of the Arid Regions of the United States*, John Wesley Powell pointed out that natural political empathies in the American West lay within the major watersheds. By cutting up the West along boundaries determined by the artificial four-square grid survey, Powell said, we were forcing our population into artificial alliances. It was a brilliant, accurate insight, and nobody paid him much attention. As a result, we have conglomerations of unlikely allies.

Montana, Wyoming: What's in a name? As Ezra Pound pointed out, nouns are not real, nothing is static; verbs and process are real. In the act of naming we are constantly involved in transmogrification, making unreal.

A friend, something of a poetic fop, once stopped in a tavern in Hailey, where Ezra was born, and asked if anybody had any idea who Pound might be. The barkeep, who looked like some kind of logging-camp Wobbly nihilist, grinned and recited:

> *Learn of the green world what can be thy place*
> *In scaled invention or true artistry*
> *Pull down thy vanity*

At least that's the story. Point is, I believe it. My friend says he fled up the road about fifteen miles, to his own kind, and happy hour at the Sun Valley Lodge.

In Boise there was a woman named Nancy Stringfellow, who spent much of her life creating one of the two or three finest bookstores between Chicago and the West Coast. She wrote, "We came here in 1914, when I was four years old. Oh, it's changed since I was a girl, but there are still little towns a girl wants to get away from and a woman wants to get back to."

In May 1982, Annick Smith and I were driving home along the upper reaches of the Lochsa River, and we elected to bide a while and ease the miseries of travel at an undeveloped wilderness spa called Jerry Johnson Hot Springs. We counted our blessings; the steaming, creekside pools were deserted.

Then we noticed a speckling of ominous gray-white residue accumulating on the rocks. It seemed to be falling from the clear sky. Have you ever been back in the western wilds, and imagined the technocratic world has ended?

Maybe it was true, the nukes had hit at last, and we were the saving remnant, alive there where the hot water bubbled at the edge of a snow-melt creek coming down from the western slopes of the Bitterroots. Maybe we were the last uncontaminated people on earth.

But it was Mount St. Helens, and we were not actually alone. In those mountains, mellowing out in other hideaway hot springs, there were many like us, seeking after something actual and vital in the touch of the world. Gary Snyder has said, "And that's the real work: to make the world real as it is and find ourselves real as we are within it."

By which he seems to mean that it is hard to believe in ourselves as real. It is commonplace to despair over children from inner-city enclaves who come to believe in nothing but moral chaos, in which notions of justice seem one contrivance after another, and the consequences of their actions appear almost perfectly arbitrary. In such situations, our lightness of being is indeed unbearable. And it's not just a dis-ease of the ghettos; it's uptown and everywhere, and those of us who can, we flee, we seek out the hot springs. We try to be at ease, and accept the grace we find.

But it seems unearned, and we are tempted to despise ourselves, even as we cultivate our decencies. It's just that it's all too easy, and so many of us are so willing to collapse into direct welcoming connection with things we claim to love, like creek-bed stones.

Mount St. Helens turned out to be disappointingly dusty, but it counted as a small apocalypse in our part of the world. That first evening, as we drove in from Jerry Johnson Hot Springs, the arc lights cast an orangey shimmering aura through the volcanic ash that was settling in small drifts along the streets of Missoula. We seized the opportunity to join a long rolling knot of party that lasted the three or four days until the rains came.

Some of us followed the action, resort to resort, Sun Valley, Boulder, Telluride, Sedona, Santa Fe, Moab, wondering where it would go next. And some of us ended up two-hearted as we could be, understanding that life breaks more easily than we imagined and trying to reconnect ourselves to the rhythms of place and family, at the same time trying to ignore the whispering of what might be actual guilt. God knows some problems were left blowing in the wind, like what about everybody else, the people we've all seen, who couldn't afford the trip?

There is a story about Paris and Gertrude Stein and Picasso and Matisse, and a migration of their followers to the American West, in search of a union between the aesthetic and the practical, and a healing connection to the natural world.

The modernist rich fall for the cowboys' native work-oriented sense of style (Oscar Wilde said the miners in Leadville were more interesting than anyone else he encountered in America, because of their floppy hats and great ground-sweeping coats), and fail to understand that cowboys and loggers and miners are rednecks at heart.

Rednecks, as they are mostly understood in the American West, tend to be working-class white folks whose people have been in the country for at least a couple of generations. They cannot be defined by class or where they grew up or profession. If one characteristic defines redneck, it is, I think, a deep sense of disenfranchisement—they feel, quite justifiably, cut off from the sources of power in their culture.

At first the modernist rich are driven to overdress as dudes or pseudo-cowboys; but they realize actual cowboys despise them, and besides, cowboys are deeply involved in unsound grazing practices that speed the destruction of the very nature that has proven to be so healing. It is a sad realization that leads to betrayal. The rich revert to ruling-class instincts and buy the land, become dude ranchers and rancher/conservationists, and everything is saved except for the cowboys.

We operate in systems of story and metaphor that we use to define the world (both natural and social) for ourselves, and we must always seek to remodel the mythology (model) we have inherited from society (because each synthesis always fails).

Artists in the American West (as everywhere), from Timothy O'Sullivan to Charlie Russell and the duck-stamp painters, to the *Baghdad Cafe* and half-buried, nose-down Cadillacs in the desert, have always worked toward helping us in that process by inciting us to witness a version of the moment with blinders off. It's what artists are for; they help us *see*; they drive society through the process of coming to fresh recognitions; it is a political responsibility.

At midmorning in the valley where the Madison River flows through southwestern Montana, the light was absolute and pure, as it would be in paradise.

Shadows cast by the mountains of the Madison Range were receding across the sagebrush foothills; a country man was baling with his New Holland hay baler.

A Montana highway patrolman smiled a good-old-boy smile when I asked about the road to the Earth First! encampment.

"Newspaper?" he said. Fifty-seven-year-old white citizen, summer haircut and a rented Toyota: Maybe I was FBI. "No," I said.

I was looking for Dave Foreman, the main spokesperson for Earth First! FBI agents had gone to his house in Tucson, showed .357 magnum pistols, and dragged him to jail wearing nothing but his shorts and handcuffs.

Now he was out on bail, awaiting trial, formally charged with conspiracy to sabotage a nuclear facility and destruction of an energy facility.

As I understood the story, it was a kind of morality play, a good man brought down by his own heedlessness. But my story wasn't working out. I had visited a charismatic leader and found him retired from charisma; I found he had never believed in charisma; he thought charismatic leaders were a step toward fascism, always had. In principle, he despised them.

There is a story about Wovoka, the Shoshone whose visions inspired the Ghost Dance Rebellion, a spiritual movement that swept across the West like a great wind, culminating in the massacre at Wounded Knee, in December 1892. A year or so later a group of plains Indians, including Sitting Bull, traveled horseback over great distances to consult with Wovoka at Walker Lake in Nevada. His wife came to the door of his ranch-hand house. "The Messiah is tired," she said, "and wishes you would all go home."

My dealings with Dave Foreman had gone like that, sort of. There was an old Volkswagen van parked alongside the gravel road, Texas plates and a bumper sticker that read *Succeed: Get the US out of Texas.*

The hippie-looking driver and his friends were stopped, talking to four flat-faced official types (we called them "haircuts" when I was a kid in the West; we were talking about deputy sheriffs).

Three rope-haired, dusty-legged young men and a woman were guarding the gate into the campground. They were a decade younger than my own children; I wondered if they were taking names.

I didn't get out of my Toyota; I didn't speak to anybody except a Forest Service ranger. "Just driving around," I said. I wondered if he wrote down my license, so some computer jockey could check the number back to Budget Rent a Car at the Jackson, Wyoming, airport, and get my name. The odor of new-cut alfalfa reminded me of childhood mornings when it was easy to know what I thought.

Who did he imagine I was? Adult citizen on a public road? Was that good enough? Was it clear I was disgusted with my government and myself and about to cause an old-fart scene? I wondered if the young people in the VW bus were being harassed, if this was harassment. I wondered if those young people were anarchist bad-asses, their names all over FBI lists; I wondered why I wasn't anything but pissed off at myself.

I don't want my name on lists. To hell with you, I thought, cursing my culture, you shouldn't get to have my name, this land belongs to me and my people, I don't need to be on your lists, I don't need your permissions, your stinking badges.

Remember those old stories about native people who were afraid to be photographed? They thought their souls were being stolen. I felt like that. There I was in the valley of the Madison River, and somebody was trying to steal my soul.

Remember grade school, when they started telling you about Manifest Destiny? Did you sense a rat? Did it ever sound like the same story you heard around the house, from adults, in which power equals wisdom.

Thomas Jefferson would have loved this agrarian wonderland at the far edge of his Louisiana Purchase, and likely thought well of these radical children. He wrote, "I hold it a little rebellion now and then is a good thing, and as necessary in the political world as storms in the physical." And, "The tree of liberty must be refreshed from time to time with the blood of patriots and tyrants."

There we were, me and all the other *haircuts*, telling ourselves we were trying to love this gorgeous morning across the world in our way, but we had actually gone tyrant. I hated my own incapacities; I hit the road; I was out of there.

Let's try one more turn at story-making. Under an early-winter moon it is possible to imagine witnessing the world in ancient clear-minded ways, without the dreaded self-conscious irony of the literate classes. There is not a single electric light in this dream. We study the stars and remember their old patterns as remnants of a language we forgot a long time ago, when the animals all knew how to lie down with one another.

In the American West our society has never been in any sense fair (our ways have been notoriously imperialistic, sexist, and racist); now our society is spinning apart (again).

Old men like my father were furious; they conspired all their lives to fashion a society that suited them. My mother was the boss's monied wife; she is confined to her bed; she watched politicians on the TV news and laughed. Those boys, she said.

The well is running dry. Where do we start this time in the continual process of remodeling ourselves and culture? How do we understand the society forming around us? What is being made?

1) The West was an enormous empty (innocent?) stage waiting for a performance. Sometimes settlers imagined it was already a paradise, but more often it was a place that needed remaking (irrigating). Malcolm Margolin, editor of *News from Native California,* likes to say Europeans found a (native American) *garden,* and turned it into a wilderness.

2) The West has been performed (written) upon; we see the history of our performance everywhere; we see our societal and personal mythologies inscribed on the landscape (fences, roads, canals, power lines, city plans, bomb ranges).

3) Many of us think much of the West has been ru-

ined. What does this mean—ruined in what sense
—ecologically, or how? Ruined in terms of what
models? By which injustices? Much that we see
(like the physical and emotional environs around
Las Vegas) resembles a kind of chaos.

In *America,* Jean Baudrillard says America is a dream. Of
course it is, life always is, we inhabit dreams. Then he says
something more interesting: He says life in the American West
is a dream of life after the crisis.

What was the crisis? "All that fascinates us is the *spectacle*
of the brain and its workings." Out West we see a society in the
midst of reinventing itself. Everyone is aware of this. We are all
watching. An ironic society is making itself up in a sometimes
quite self-reflexive way.

Our crisis is psychological, a crisis of awareness and guilt
(through greed, we have ruined our paradise; we knew we were
doing it) which has driven us to a deep sense of powerlessness.

Anomie is the easy result (all that counts in the long run is
selfishness; I watch myself watch myself; all actions are equal—
too many drugs). In response to this crisis of will a society we
don't understand is evolving with terrific speed (inscribing itself on us and our landforms).

Out of control (again), as in our semi-genocidal history of
conquest and settlement. What to do? Maybe we want to live
inside a new story, but how do we define it, how do we choose
it, how can we make it come to be?

On our first visit together in Glacier Park, Annick and I and her
twin boys, Alex and Andrew, (they were about eleven at the

time) hiked some six miles up to the Sperry Chalet, a 3,700-foot rise in elevation from the paved parking lot at the McDonald Lake Lodge. The boys ranged ahead like wolves when word came down the hill that we were in danger of missing supper.

The second day we traipsed over to the Sperry Glacier, only about four miles and a 1,500-foot rise in elevation; it was like walking in the pastures of heaven. The twins ran their eleven-year-old routes. Annick and I rested on the cool glacial ice.

For a while we didn't notice the condom. It had been used and tossed away, collapsed, slippery, and luminous in the morning; someone had been testing our ice; couples wandered the glacier; Annick wondered who it could have been—them, or them? I wondered exactly how much self-absorbed theatricality had been involved. It was my way of condescending to the moment.

Sometimes we live to see a single thing light up. When I am hounded and strange, looking to hide and perfect my revenge (my living well), then I cleave to obsessive purity, a place to be, where nothing is forgiven.

Above the treeline in the stony highlands it is possible to imagine the absolute clarity of crystalline light over the glacial cirques is a moral imperative: Be correct—it is a way of killing possibility. We should go out under the blue-white skies, throw down a blanket and make love on the glaciers (and carry out the parts that are not biodegradable).

We are a far way into devastation of the interwoven system of life on our planet—the single environment in which our race will ever be able to live. Many of us are seeking ways to stop that devastation; we think it is an enterprise of uttermost urgency. We at least think we are trying to save the world, which is a particularly powerful way of saving ourselves.

We are reinventing our notion of what is most valuable to us, as individuals and as a species, redefining what we take to be sacred; it is our most urgent business, our major communal enterprise. We are deeply afraid of trying to exist on some starship, alone in the universe; we refuse to go on with business as usual.

If we have some luck, we want to believe (and why not?), and if we stay as smart as we can, we may someday find ourselves living inside the solace of a coherent self. Miners and cowhands and unmarried mothers and married mothers and insurance salesmen and old woman tattoo artists and nature freaks and timber fallers and everyday downtown drunks and so on unto glory, we must learn empathy (we tell ourselves), and cherish and forgive each other.

A young man went to an abandoned house where he had lived with his family, and found a bird trapped inside the empty white-painted rooms, batting at the windows. The sunny spaces where he had run to his mother as a child were thick with this terror. Even when he opened the windows, and the bird escaped, there was no cure.

Imagine a life in which the meadowlarks and magpies come down from their trees and look in our windows at night and study us in our sleep, and then fly away, thinking tomorrow we must talk and sing to them because nothing else ever helps.

PART THREE

Departures

1

On spring days in western Montana, as you approach St. Ignatius on the Flathead Indian Reservation, you can find yourself stunned by the glittering alpine peaks in the Mission Mountains Wilderness, fresh snow and perpetual glaciers against a perfect bluebird sky. In the valley below, along Post Creek, the willows are opening new leaves, and the hayfields are greening up. It can be understood as a vision of paradise.

"Except," I heard a rancher say, "for the goddamned grizzly bears. How'd you like to live where the grizzlies come down off the mountain to eat apples in your orchard?" Paradise, for some, does not mean wilderness, particularly when they are raising small children who love to run and play in the orchard. It means killing grizzlies with a high-powered rifle, and some righteous soul does, every few seasons, in an orchard at the foot of the Mission Mountains, where the ancient West and our 1990s homeland border on one another.

The little city where I live, Missoula, lies south of the Missions, at the conjunction of river valleys where the Big Blackfoot River and the Bitterroot River join the Clark's Fork of the Columbia. Rattlesnake Creek, which flows through the middle of town, originates in a Wilderness Area a few miles outside the city limits. So much water, such fly-fishing, so close to home. And no grizzlies.

In the northern Rockies we often have a week or so of rain over the September equinox. The nights go to freezing. The air seems cleansed. We walk into distances turned faintly golden, implying connection to paradise, and eternity.

Western larch are dropping their golden needles on the mountain slopes above the Big Blackfoot River. Translucent yellow aspen leaves flutter in the touch of a breeze I cannot feel, and quiet themselves. The sky is perfect doll-baby blue, and cool.

The world is at its most beautiful, and it's time for the fall ritual of Going Out, the point of which is forgetting yourself and falling away into moments of intimacy. It's not a soft-headed option; if we get far enough out of touch with the feel and smell and taste and look of things we can go crazy.

People like me are particularly vulnerable. The days ring with intimation that it's almost time to get indoors to what I think of as a carpentered life, living in rooms, in artificial light, focusing our eyes down to indoor work. My friends are beginning to die from the wear of their lives. I could die before I taste the autumn air again. It is a crazy-making notion.

Each fall, contact comes in some different way. Last year it was a badger, outside its burrow under the foundation of what was once a log barn on the bluff above the river, the animal squat and poised, a fierce and fearless creature, and nothing I expected to see. I have a history of bad killer karma with badgers.

When I was a rancher, badgers dug their burrows in my levee banks, and the levee banks washed away. The carrots soaked in strychnine turned luminous orange. I dropped them in burrows, at that work in rubber gloves, fearing for myself.

About that same time, out on the high sagebrush plains we called desert in southeastern Oregon, near a stock-watering tank fed by a slow windmill, I drove up in my pickup and caught a badger in the open and vulnerable. I wounded him with a .22 pistol, and he did the thing I never imagined an animal doing, angry and wounded or not. He charged. I ran for my pickup truck and dived in the box, just ahead of his rage. He hissed, and I raised the pistol but didn't shoot again.

What was I doing? Why had I shot him in the first place? Was it just that he was an animal and I was not? Was it just that I had power over him? What was he hurting, what was I proving? Was it just that he was strange? Was I trying to weed the world of strangeness? Did owning the lives of other creatures help me ignore the fact of my own inevitable and oncoming death? Was it that simple-minded and stupid?

While I certainly did not ask myself such questions at the time, they were there, needing answers—in the confusions of that moment when I did not shoot the badger again, as in so many other such moments during that time, when, for instance, I did not kill the mallards that rose clamoring into the morning sky before my shotgun (I had been stalking them for an hour), when I proved able to acknowledge that I just wanted to see them up close, and not kill them. Though I didn't know it yet, I was turning from what had been my life, and from the idea that I was fit to own some of the earth in any absolute way. The point of things, I was beginning to sense, is cherishing, not owning.

Maybe that badger died in its burrow, alone and in agony

from the wound I inflicted. I prefer to think it healed and lived to an ancient badger age.

Upstream near the Continental Divide men have discovered gold. Someday they may pile up the marginal ore and spray it with cyanide to leach out the last precious remnants. Maybe some of the poison will find its way into the river, and drift downstream to the badger and me.

The light shimmered with clarity so absolute everything seemed on the verge of going grainy and dissolving, grainy like some pointillist painting, seeming to come at us in slants like the sky might be scattered with mirrors and prisms. One of my reasons for living in Montana is the light in October.

If I could manage it, I might truly realize that the western larch and the scree slopes have the same life that I do. But actually healing back into nature seems impossible. Maybe I find it so because I understand that everything is built of stories, and to some degree imaginary.

Maybe we have all become too many selves. Maybe that's the point of going out, trying to get back to an ancient single-minded creature inside us, which we imagine as unthinking and wedded to actuality.

The badger turns and vanishes down his burrow. I am alone in the ringing light above the Big Blackfoot River. My memories of that animal, poised and motionless, are a form of sustenance, to feed my imagination as I try to imagine myself healed to glory of things.

Montana reaches six hundred miles from remnants of modified maritime cedar-tree forests near the Idaho border to the meeting of the Missouri and the Yellowstone Rivers near the North Dakota border, and it splits into two kingdoms, divided north and south along the front range of the Rockies. If state boundaries had been laid out in the sensible way John Wesley Powell called for, along watershed lines, Montana would be two states, each a more coherent community.

Western Montana is a land of alpine mountains and pretty farmland valleys, Yellowstone and Glacier National Parks, and great wilderness areas. In the Beartooth-Absaroka Wilderness along the northern edge of Yellowstone Park people hike for days above 10,000 feet in elevation, on trails through great blue and yellow fields of delicate wildflowers. The waters of glacial tarns mirror snowfields on stony peaks. In autumn you can horse pack into the Bob Marshall Wilderness along the rockies front, and photograph rutting, bugling elk in natural meadows beside the Sun River. Some claim there are more elk in that country than there were when Lewis and Clark came by a hundred and ninety years ago. They claim the rockies front is the largest recovering big game range in the world. It's sad, to me, that we only know how to talk about those animals as "game."

We go into wilderness, I think, to renew our intimacy with

a world that is natural and perhaps sacred. To me, sacred means necessary. We evolved in nature, with other animals (think of them as our companions in the vast universe). Isolate us from nature too long, as individuals, as societies, and we start getting nervous, crazy, unmoored, inhabited by dis-eases we cannot name, driven to thoughtless ambitions and easy cruelties. This is not, I think, sappy talk, or overstated. It's only true. We feel it, we see it everywhere, every morning in the newspaper, so many gone so frantic.

Contact with the natural world is an experience that comes to us like a gift in Montana; we look up and find ourselves in some kind of intimacy with things as they have always been in the history of our species. It is a main reason many of us stay forever.

In eastern Montana the short-grass plains roll across enormous distances of seemingly infinite variety. I go out into the beauty of frozen winter landscapes between towns like Jordan and Circle and rivers like the Musselshell and the Tongue, hear the silence ringing, and sense that the thronging world is not so overcrowded after all. I stand by a fenceline in the shimmering of summer heat over white houses and red barns isolated amid the yellow wheatland and fallow plow-ground strips alternating across the country northeast of Great Falls, and I romance myself with the idea that it's a place where I could settle into dreams while the world went on without my troubles. In that country, follow back roads, and carry a well-stocked cooler. You may end up beguiled but a long way from provisions.

Montana is a place where independence and minding your own business tend to be regarded as prime virtues. Many of the people who came wanted to escape what they saw as the cramping and compromises involved in inhabiting, as one successful escapee put it, "the more thickly populated dens of society." Many came seeking to redefine themselves in a new life. I was one of them.

In 1969, at the age of thirty-six, on the run, I lucked into a job teaching at the University of Montana, and a home in a town with a tradition of fine writing (Leslie Fiedler, Richard Hugo, James Crumley, James Welch, so many others since then). And, most important, among people delighted to see me be whatever I could manage. Self-realization (but not necessarily conventional success) is considered another prime virtue.

Montana is mainly little settlements and societies, many rough-edged and isolated, held together by self-respect, hard-handed individualism, and not much money. When I'm on the road in Montana, I like to stop and have a drink and some talk with the locals in country taverns like the Jersey Lily in Ingomar, out on the plains north of the Yellowstone River, good people who are inclined to be open-minded and irreverent, witty and maybe a little condescending toward anyone so foolish as to live full-time in the vicinity of cities.

"But you got to get around, all the same," an old man told me. "I go to Seattle I could eat them oysters three meals a day." He stared off toward the horizon. I wondered if he was seeing a dozen freshly cracked belugas on the half-shell, and I agreed.

If you are inclined to understand us, visit the old women and retired hard-rock miners in Butte, which was once the empire city of western mining. Imagine the courage it took to go down to your work in the terrible darkness of the deep shafts, as much as seven thousand feet under the surface, shift after shift (or the powerful hearts of women who lived their lives with such men). My favorite Butte taverns are the Helsinki (near the Berkeley Pit, the huge open-pit mine at the edge of downtown), where they send drinks to the sauna on a dumbwaiter, and the M&M, where the waitresses color their hair and fingernails green on St. Patrick's Day. Butte is another part of the natural world.

Montana history has been one of resettlement after resettlement, haunted by Old-West violence. After the pressure of white settlement drove them from their forested homelands to the north and west of the Great Lakes, the Sioux and Cheyenne and Blackfeet and Crow drifted to the plains east of the Rocky Mountains. Fur trappers and buffalo hunters followed, and the United States military. After decades of hideously genocidal warfare (it's claimed, and believed, that white traders gave the Blackfeet smallpox with a gift of infected blankets), the Indians were confined to reservations. They had to make way for the gold-camp miners and cattlemen from Texas and railroaders from Chicago and wave after wave of homesteaders from Europe, each seeking possibility and freedom. Some of the white folks stayed and made a killing, more starved out and left. And some stayed anyway, however tough it got.

Montana has been an economic colony ever since the beaver trade. Our traditional sources of revenue have been shipping timber, minerals, wool, butcher livestock, and wheat for the population centers in the East (and, lately, Japan). Gold, cedar logs, copper, petroleum—we have always suffered the whims of a boom-or-bust export economy.

Montana politics have always been driven by that fact. And, just as importantly, by the warfare between working stiffs and out-of-state corporations that characterized the early days in Butte, which for many decades existed as an economic fiefdom of the copper monopoly called the Anaconda Company. A feel for this history can help you make sense of and partway forgive the sometimes deeply xenophobic attitudes in Montana. We've been driven to suspect the motives of monied outsiders; we take care of the home folks first. Montana politicians are careful to show vital concern about the well-being of wage-earning citizens. We don't, for instance, have a sales tax, which is understood as a way of preying on the poor.

Along the way Montana has suffered vast ecological damage (the Clark Fork drainage between Butte and Missoula is the largest SuperFund toxic-waste cleanup site in the country). Our timberlands are mostly logged, our mines are closing, our farmers and ranchers are sharing sad economic times with all of American agriculture, and we're engaged in unhappy debate as to which of our roadless areas should be dedicated to wilderness and which should be left for logging. This argument is commonly seen in Montana as a conflict between out-of-state environmentalists, and equally out-of-state timber and mining corporations. The sympathies of local citizens seem about evenly split, often depending on their source of income. "You can't eat the scenery."

Visit the logging country around Libby in the fall, when larch on the evergreen slopes have turned golden along with the leaves of aspen and cottonwood on the Bull River, below the Cabinet Mountain Wilderness Area. Talk to timber fallers and millworkers whose canvas Carhart coveralls are rank with sawdust and sweat. See what they think about environmental issues, and attempt to balance the beauty of nature all around you against the dismay of people who face the prospect of losing their jobs, maybe their town. You'll understand the dilemma. People are frightened, broke. We are being driven to new notions of who we are, and how we might make a living. We know we are privileged to live as we do, with our freedoms, and we don't want to give them up.

People whose forefathers took the land from the Indians now confront the same fate. They are furious, thinking everything their people fought and suffered for, over generations, will be taken away.

And they may be right. But perhaps not all is lost. Recently I traveled in the Dordogne, in the heartland of France, a region sometimes thick with tourists. Local culture, and agriculture, seem to be thriving. The same is true in Tuscany and Umbria, areas of Italy that have been farmed for more than two thousand years, and for centuries settled and resettled by the rich and privileged, visited by the streams of tourists drawn by the artistic treasures in Florence and Siena and Assisi.

Clearly it is possible to combine stewardship for the land, a rooted way of local life, with an economy benefiting in some major ways from tourism and wealthy settlers. We need to consider such models as we try to define our future in Montana, always keeping before us, of course, the fact that we are inexorably moving toward a more class-bound society.

In the meantime, we can still go visit in places like the sweet little town of Augusta, on the Sun River just east of the rockies front, where the prairies begin. I used to go there in late June, for the rodeo, when the great cottonwoods are in full leaf over the short grassy trail from the single block of downtown stores and taverns to the arena. World champion cowboys fly in to compete with locals. You see their aircraft landing on the meadowland airstrip not far away. They ride in Augusta in the afternoon, fly out and ride that night under the arc lights in some other town, like Cody, Wyoming. I always tried to sit near the chutes, where the mud flies.

But people have been saying rodeo is just another of the animal-taunting sports, like cock-fighting, and there seems to be some truth in the notion. So I don't go any more. Nobody misses me. People in places like Augusta don't care much for my bi-coastal anxieties.

Up the Blackfoot River my true companion, Annick Smith, lives in a big log house. We stand out on her porch on a summer morning, leaning on the rail, with a long view to timbered hills, at ease in this fine kingdom, musing on golf in the late afternoon and on friends, wine, a few trout for dinner.

Such serenities can lead us to believe we have located a place where serious harm might never come. We understand that we are privileged. Have we escaped to hidden lives behind our mountains, have we skipped on our responsibilities to the so-called Great World and its discontents? Probably, to some degree anyway. We wonder if it is possible to go on getting away with life in this home-child heaven, this good place. The answer, at least for today, seems to be yes, for a while, if we stay smart, and take care, give something back, all of us.

3

And time has whittled down the cabbage leaves to thin white wings.
Brian Patten, *"Through the Tall Grass in Your Head"*

I've spent a morning fishing the streams along the White River Syncline in the Bob Marshall Wilderness, and in the afternoon stood looking down on the wilderness elk pastures along the Sun River from the overthrust escarpment of the Chinese Wall. We search for morels under the cottonwoods along sandbars by the Clark Fork River, play golf in the afternoon, go sit on a terrace overlooking the lights of Missoula while getting into the grapefruit juice and Herendura, and sleep at home with the door unlocked. People ask why I live in Montana. I give them answers like that. They're kind of true.

Montana has been called a small town with long streets. A friend who lives east over the Continental Divide talks about falling in with "psychic spooks," and driving the prairies for days. "It doesn't do anything for my religious situation," he said, "but it's so beautiful I kind of forget."

That's some of what we like to think we're doing here, learning to enjoy the solace of connection to infinities. But infinities can be too infinite. Radical freedoms can translate into utter isolation.

Crossing the Rockies at Marias Pass, beside the Northern Pacific tracks along the southern edge of Glacier Park, in October, while it was spitting snow, I saw a moose come to the edge of the asphalt, and gallop away, swift, huge-headed and spooky like a horse. I was dropping toward East Glacier, where generations of tourists got off Pullman cars to be greeted by Blackfeet Indians wearing authentic bead-work costumes.

Beyond were the wind-blown reservation towns where the Blackfeet actually live, and east of them lay the dryland farming country known as the "Golden Triangle," alternate strips of crop and fallow ground. Winter wheat is planted in the fall, sprouts, lies dormant through the cold months, and starts growing again in the spring. It is harvested in midsummer, and it is the primary dollar crop in Montana (in 1924 the northeastern Montana town of Scobey was the largest wheat-loading center in North America).

Out on those farmer plains we are in the land of ICBM silos and blizzards, shimmering summertime, tight white-painted farmsteads, elaborate windbreak treelines, and millionaires (an economically viable wheat farm is worth at least a million). It can be understood as a land of monocultures, both agricultural and spiritual.

Cutbank, Shelby, Chester, Kremlin, Havre, Chinook, Harlem, Malta, Wolf Point, Poplar: the towns string south of the Canadian border on a route called "the high-line." Distances between them are dictated by concerns like getting crops to the railroad. Their names embody patterns of ethnic settlement and history like a teaching poem about the mix of culture that might have been: Native American, German-Russian, Dutch, Mediterranean, wolf-hunter.

East of Malta, in the twilight, I saw what looked to be a boy and a girl, one long-haired and the other not, wind-burned faces, skinny ranch kids in their after-school clothes, carrying damp burlap sacks to cover the late crops against frost in the night. I recall my own childhood with perfect precision, my father's garden and the stinking burlap. I sulked during those hours covering the cucumbers; darkness came down, bearing the cold.

I wondered if those children outside Malta felt as distant as I had. Maybe their feelings of insignificance are even more overpowering; I didn't grow up with television and the sight of taillights feathering away into the darkness.

". . . the party killed 3 beaver and a deer. We can send out at any time and obtain whatever species of meat the country affords in as large a quantity as we wish."

—Meriwether Lewis

On May 8, 1805, William Clark climbed a rise on the north side of the Missouri River. The downstream country, looking back toward the Dakotas, in the words of his companion, Meriwether Lewis, was "level and beautiful on both sides of the river, with large herds of buffalo distributed throughout."

From the place where Clark stood, above the highway, I could see bottomland farms (no wolves, no buffalo, nothing wild but varmints and waterfowl and occasional chaos in the soul).

Upstream lay the intricately eroded territory of the Missouri badlands, with its white cliffs, where the river and its tributaries cut an impossibly complex watershed through a great highlands plateau. Sunlight reflected off the quarter-million-acre lake (134 miles long, 1,520 miles of shoreline) backed up by the largest earth-fill structure on the planet (126 million cubic yards), the Fort Peck Dam.

William Clark, if he had seen such waters, might have thought they were an arm of some undiscovered ocean. In the Cambrian period, 570 million years Before Present, great waters covered the plains. As they rose and fell over millennia an explosion of multicellular life died and was buried on the mud flats. Strange examples are preserved in the so-called Burgess Shale found high in the Canadian Rockies, north of Banff, a town where the citizens have taken to putting up their street signs in both English and Japanese (for Pacific Rim tourists).

Five hundred or so million years later (70 million years Before Present), in the Cretaceous period, another sea washed beaches in the high plains country. It was the Age of Dinosaurs; the Rockies were rising. The dinosaurs migrated to nest on high ground along the rockies front (eggs have been found, with baby duckbills inside, just east of Choteau, Montana).

In 1902 an expedition from the American Museum, led by a man named Barnum Brown, went to Montana and found, in what is known as the Hell Creek sandstone formation in the Missouri River badlands, something nobody had ever seen, remains of the great carnivorous *Tyrannosaurus rex*, our terrible-toothed forty-foot, eight-ton comic-book "King of the tyrant lizards." Of four resurrected *tyrannosaurus* skeletons on display in American museums, all were found in the vicinity of

Garfield County, Montana, a fact that generates great local pride.

The five-turbine power-house/surge tower at the Fort Peck dam is a structure of such 1930s monumental scale it might be imagined as a lost remnant of some heroic civilization (maybe it is). In the museum at the base there is a huge three-horned skull of a *tricopterous*. Just beyond through soundproof windows, in a metallic powerhouse control room, a man sat watching banks of motionless dials. It was the perfect metaphor, our interwoven biological past sealed off from the shadowless future.

> *Paradise lies all around. Can you not see it?*
> —Gnostic parable

Jordan, Montana (population 485), is frighteningly isolated by any downtown standard—they have a hospital but the nearest doctor is ninety miles away in Miles City. The woman at the motel asked if I was a paleontologist.

That night in the Hell Creek Bar a handsome adult woman wanted to dance to the jukebox but I wouldn't. Nobody else was dancing and I was in the presence of ranchland people: quiet men; Indian women keeping their own company; an over-dressed courting couple, trying it out in public; three mid-career gents wearing expensive boots (cow buyers or bankers or government employees who were talking a lot, too hearty but tolerated); a lank teenaged boy in tennis shoes who was watching his father as his father drank.

There was a time when I belonged in places like that, but

since I quit the ranch business, I was sure those people could spot me for a defector. I wanted to sulk in the corner and keep quiet like a spy.

A hundred and fifty years ago some sixty million buffalo were roaming the North American prairies. The last wild ones were shot out south of Jordan in 1886, by William Hornaday, a taxidermist, for display in the Smithsonian. He went back to Washington, DC, with twenty-four hides, sixteen skeletons, and fifty-one skulls. It was his nineteenth-century way of preserving the last wild buffalo.

Frank and Deborah Popper have proposed to restore them. Sociologists at Rutgers, they have done a lot of homework in ten Great Plains states between the 98th meridian and the Rocky Mountains, seeking what Deborah Popper calls "distressed areas," counties "that have lost at least 50 percent of population since 1930. An over-10-percent loss between 1980 and 1988. Four or fewer people per square mile. High median age. Twenty percent or more in poverty."

A lot of counties qualify. The Poppers say such areas should not have been settled in the first place. They propose a 139,000-square-mile national grasslands, which would include a lot of the western Dakotas, western Nebraska, eastern Montana, and areas in Kansas, Oklahoma, Texas, Colorado, New Mexico, and Wyoming. This entity would be called the "Buffalo Commons," (aka "Big Open"), and, according to theory, be biodiversity-enshrined. Citizens who live there could make a good living off hunters and the tourist trade. Everybody wins.

This is nightmare talk to long-time inhabitants of the short-grass plains; it's an old story. In his 1878 annual report for the United States Geologic Survey, John Wesley Powell said flatly that the shortgrass plains could never be adapted to intensive cropping because of inadequate rainfall and recurrent drouth. His report was ignored. By 1910 James Hill had built his Great Northern Railroad across the Montana highline, and he was trying to sell tickets, claiming 320 acres would support a homestead farm; settlers came to the plains bearing possessions; it was a mass migration; they built shacks, they tried to farm, most of them failed, most of them left, having wasted years in dirt-eating poverty.

Most citizens of Jordan are descendants of the survivors, and now they find social scientists talking about turning their homeland into a preserve for wild beasts; they are understandably angry and humiliated.

They think the environmentalists value the goddamned buffalo more than they value the sacrifices of their people. I imagined telling people in Jordan that I thought the Buffalo Commons held at least the seed of a necessary idea. It is our duty, I would tell them, as the dominant species, to preserve huge tracts of land in something resembling its native condition. The biological interactions necessary to ensure the continuities of life are astonishingly complex, and cannot take place in little islands of semi-wilderness like the national parks.

I imagined saying, "We're taking your land, we're kicking you out, we're sorry, but our purposes are larger than yours." I imagined telling them we need to replant the world and make it holy again; I imagined talking about the mental health of our species.

It is good for our sanity to witness nature at its most multitudinous; such encounters function in our imaginations as a sight of possibility—dinosaurs and on to life everlasting. I imagined telling those people that we continue to inhabit an age of sacred beasts, even as we destroy them.

No doubt I would be dismissed as another nitwit missionary, come to take everything they had suffered for. It's easy, amid such distances as in eastern Montana, where the major rhythms of life have not changed for generations, to find you are estranged from the national mood. The people in Jordan think they have good reason to go xenophobic, and not so much fear strangers as despise them.

Talking about the Buffalo Commons would probably be a good way to get your ass kicked in a place like the Hell Creek Bar in Jordan, Montana.

But maybe not. Maybe those good people would tell me paradise is all around. Maybe they would tell me to take a walk into the world. I did, the next morning. I saw a broom-tailed red fox on the outskirts of Jordan. A great blue heron flew under the highway bridge and came out on the other side.

The essential American soul is hard, isolate, stoic, and a killer.
—D.H. Lawrence

In the fur-trapper days, it is said, Indian women were so incessantly raped by white men that they developed a strategy called "going for the sand." When the trappers showed up those women would go to the creeks and pack their vaginas with sand.

In January, 1870, the temperature 40 below, Major Eugene Baker and his Second US Cavalry massacred a friendly band of Blackfeet-Piegan camped on the Marias River, their lodges full of smallpox victims. One hundred and seventy-three Indians died; survivors agreed to settle on the reservation.

James Welch, the Blackfeet writer, tells of searching out the Marias massacre site while doing research for his novel *Fool's Crow*, in which the massacre is the pivotal event. It wasn't marked at all, he says, it was just an open field by the river. The site of the Custer massacre is a National Monument; we celebrate our history in disingenuous ways.

Welch says he drove on, from Montana into Canada, into the sacred sandhills of the Blackfeet (they were covered with dune buggy tracks). "They believed you would go live in the sandhills after you died. It would be much like your present life, traveling with your people, and hunting."

The Blackfeet, it seems, believed they lived someplace close to heaven already. They believed life was supposed to be the way it already was.

During the terrible winter of 1883–84, they were abandoned by their federal agent, out of food and too weak to hunt. Rescue missions found the living mad with hunger and grief, wolves in their lodges, tearing at the flesh of the unburied. Six hundred had starved to death—a quarter of the tribe.

Woody Kipp tells me a parable about life on the Blackfeet Reservation. "In the old days, out by Four Horns Lake, there was a hole in the ground. A man named Jack Miller tried to find the bottom. He went down 400 feet on a rope, and came out saying it was bottomless.

"The old Blackfeet stayed away. They thought it was a route where spirits came and went. In the 1930s, somebody said their cows were falling in, so the CCC [Civilian Conservation Corps] capped it over with cement."

Woody is a man I met in 1970; he was just out of the Marines, back from Vietnam, and trying to write; a lot of what we did in those days was drink; years got away. Woody went back to the Blackfeet Reservation; he lived where the plains begin, near the native town of Heart Butte, hauled house water with a wagon, steamed himself in the sweat lodges, and rediscovered Blackfeet spirituality. Now he's back at the University of Montana, his hair in traditional braids, writing editorials for the student newspaper.

"Right now," Woody says, "on this issue, we're working with environmentalists. But they'll pull out when it's settled. There's nobody to count on but ourselves."

Woody is talking about preserving the de facto wilderness of the Badger–Two Medicine Area on the western edge of the reservation (123,000 acres, the largest unprotected roadless area in the Greater Glacier Ecosystem). A coalition of Blackfeet traditionalists and environmental groups claim the Badger–Two Medicine area is a "traditional cultural property" worthy of designation to the National Register of Historic Places.

Dan Boggs, chairman of the tribal land board says, "We want to save what we've got. We've still got the scars and scabs of the past. . . . It is our belief the earth does not belong to us. We belong to the earth." People who died during the starvation winter are buried up there.

"Spotted Eagle, Scarface, Bullshoe," Woody Kipp says, "those mountains are religious sites. The Badger–Two Medicine is our spiritual homeland."

You wonder what he means. Something, I would guess, about quieting your sensibilities and allowing yourself to see and smell and touch the earth, finding yourself in dreams, going to the mountains and encouraging those dreams, studying them as mirrors in which you see yourself in connection to holiness.

But others on the Blackfeet Reservation see a different

equation: money for the desperately poor. Oil companies want to begin exploration in the Badger–Two Medicine Area, and they think the reservation is due the prosperous times that would come with a strike (and surely they are due, but the chances of a commercial field are one in a thousand).

Economic development is hard to come by on Montana reservations, despite the work of men like State Representative Bob Gervais of Browning. "It's the old story," he says. "If there was any oil money it wouldn't stick around here for long. We have to fight the whites every step of the way. We have to hire lawyers, and attack. The reservations need to raise their own money. We have to control our own fates. We have to educate our people. We have to beat the whites at their own game."

On a snowy morning in Browning I saw a knot of men shuffling and blowing their noses as they told jokes in the parking lot in front of a liquor store, waiting for the doors to open. So many wake up drunk so much of the time; fetal alcohol syndrome is an urgent health problem on reservations all over the West. In the summer of 1985, on the Wind River Reservation of Wyoming (Arapaho and Shoshone, population somewhere near 5,000) a series of nine young men, ages fourteen to twenty-five, killed themselves. Scott Swistowicz, a teacher at St. Stephen's Indian School, said, "I think the futility of what they saw in their futures became overwhelming."

People at Wind River responded by staging healing ceremonies. They began relearning their traditional languages; the old culture was all they had. It's working. Gary Collins, an Arapaho tribal leader, said, "We have decided to determine where the river will flow. When you look at history you see that the societies which thrive are the ones that control their own destinies. That's what we have to do."

It's going to be a tough climb. The situation on most reservations is roughly that of inner-city residents; there is no work, and thus no way to connect into a society as essentially heartless as ours. Eleven organized Indian tribes live in Montana; we have seven reservations. There is no way up, no ladder to climb. It is absolutely necessary, in Montana and all over the West, if we want to admire ourselves and proceed into the future with some belief in our power to heal our society, that we start paying our debts to them, to the degree that we can. We must encourage them as they seek to honor their own communities, and help them build economies that are centered in their cultures, and completely theirs. We don't so much need a war on drugs and alcohol in America, we need a war on anomie and powerlessness.

It is the proper work of our national leaders to bring us to confrontation against our own coldheartedness. That they have not done so is the major political failure of our time. We are essentially leaderless, and learning to forget our dream of a just society. In embracing our selfishness, we ultimately learn to despise ourselves; it will be the death of our society.

"Stranger, you're driving your ducks to a mighty poor pond."
    —overheard at the rail in the Eastgate Liquor Lounge

I stopped off the highway in the deep-shaft mining town of Wallace, Idaho (the only stoplight on I-90 between Boston and

Seattle). The elegant old hotel barroom was empty except for a heavy-shouldered man down the line a couple of stools; he was drunk; his legs had been amputated above the knee. "What I got for it," he said, "was notched."

He had to be talking about a lifetime given to the mines; he was furious; he grasped the bar with his huge broken-fingered hands, lifted himself, and started coming after me like a crab, suspended on those terrible, quivering forearms, tattoos knotting, his anger so justifiable and futile.

For decades Butte was the largest, richest city between Denver and the coast. Butte was whores and gambling and knockabout violence; Butte was also families, ethnic neighborhoods, and fraternal societies.

But mostly Butte was the Anaconda Company, the great copper monopoly that effectively ran Montana at its pleasure into the sixth decade of this century. Copper ore was reduced on wood and charcoal fires in open-hearth smelters; the city lived under toxic yellow smoke. Sulfuric acid dripping from the walls in 2,700 miles of tunneling burned the miners' clothes and flesh; silicosis was epidemic. In the beginning the "copper kings" battled for possession of Butte, then they sold it out in 1906, to eastern interests.

On June 8, 1917, a carbide lamp ignited a fire at the 2,400-foot level; the shaft was a roaring downdraft chimney; this was the Speculator Mine Disaster; 164 miners died. Three days later miners and smeltermen organized the Metal Mine Workers' Union. On June 29, 1917, 15,000 men in Butte, Anaconda, and Great Falls went on strike. On the night of August 17, 1917, IWW organizer Frank Little was dragged four miles down the railroad track to a trestle and hanged by "parties unknown." A message was pinned to his shirt: "Others take notice. First and last warning." By mid-winter the strike was over; the Anaconda Company won. In 1920 company guards fired into workers in Anaconda (one died). By 1921 Butte had been under martial law six times.

In 1955 open-pit mining began. By the time it was abandoned, the Berkeley Pit had 2,500 miles of road, it was 1,500 feet deep, and it had swallowed 3 square miles, edging toward the heart of the city. In 1968 1,700 miners lost their jobs after a nine-month strike. In 1981 the Anaconda Company was bought by the Atlantic Richfield Company (ARCO). On April 23, 1982, ARCO stopped pumping; the Berkeley Pit began filling with water rich in lead, arsenic, manganese, copper, cadmium, zinc, and sulfates at the rate of about 2½ feet per month. Those contaminants will be seeping into the Butte water supply, and the Clark Fork River, which flows past Missoula to the Columbia and Portland and the Pacific, before long.

The scenario holds for deep mines abandoned over all the Rockies: pumping stops, the water rises, contamination works its ways into streams which flow down to rivers, which flow down to cities. Nobody knows what to do.

But Butte is recovering. They let go of the old killer past. It must have been hard. When I went down to the M&M bar, the joint was thick with men and women who had long ago decided to gamble their lives on the fate of the working class.

"Let's toast the company," one of them said. He bought a couple of shots of Irish. We held them to the light; his fingers were thick with broken calluses. "Fuck the company," he shouted, and we tossed them back. He cackled with happiness.

The tough, as we know, move on. "Butte," the writer Thomas McGuane told me, "can be thought of as the vibe center of Montana. The people in Butte were entitled to a great sense of defeat. They responded with humor and imagination. It is our best model in Montana, if we want to enjoy the future at all."

When ARCO closed the mines, Butte was dying. In 1986 the Butte Local Development Corporation helped put together a $12 million package that got 300 miners back to work. But that wasn't enough to drive an economic comeback.

Business and labor people got together, and agreed to sit on ancient hatreds. With start-up funding from the Montana Power Company, and expertise from the Montana College of Mineral Science and Technology, one of the finest mining schools in the nation, they founded a series of high-tech institutes like the National Center for Appropriate Technology, and Entech, which markets hazardous waste expertise.

They got smart and moved beyond lamentation and powerless nostalgia to participation in the international network of technologies, inevitably part of our future. And they did it as a community. It's no accident our most creative and humane politicians, Mike Mansfield and Pat Williams, came out of a town as streetwise as Butte.

"I mean, what the hell, she's ruined anyhow."
—overheard in the laundromat

Miles City evolved into the great nineteenth-century cow town on the northern plains. You catch a sense of that old glory in the Montana Bar: stamped tin ceiling, hand-laid Italian tile, the heads of a red-haired longhorn and a buffalo looking down, and in the front window, a full-mounted Audubon big-horn sheep.

The first Audubon big-horn was sighted on April 29, 1805, near what is now Culberston, Montana, by Joseph Fields of the Lewis and Clark expedition; the last one was killed on Seven Blackfoot Creek in the Missouri Breaks in April 1916.

Dinosaurs, buffalo, grizzlies, old growth forests—it's a story that tells us we inhabit a dying place. It becomes an excuse for giving in to selfishness (most of us don't listen when somebody says the Indians were living sort of right in the first place, in communal cultures and a sustaining relationship with the potentialities of their homeland).

Our mythological stories in the West, from *The Big Sky* and *Shane* to *The Wild Bunch* and *Chinatown* and *Melvin and Howard*, have always swung on the subject of easy money. Just like so many real Western adventures.

Last fall I visited a fourth-generation eastern Montana rancher named Wally McRae at his place on Rosebud Creek, where Custer passed by on his way to oblivion at the Little Big Horn. McRae was furious with the business community in Miles City.

"They're embarrassed," he said, "by their cowboy heritage. They want big business. They want to import garbage from the East."

It's true, the idea has been seriously proposed, and so-called regional landfills may eventually come into being, coal trains going east, and sometimes hazardous waste coming west by the trainload from various seaports. Montana wants trade, and there's lots of open space.

McRae is something of a media figure (a cowboy poet, he is a 1989 winner of a National Folklife Award), but in many ways he is like my father, both an innovator and traditionalist; he collects old-time photographs and tack, he has sheds filled with retired horsedrawn equipment. On the day I visited, McRae was dusty and tired from a morning spent getting his horses ready to take over to the Tongue River country where his roundup would begin; his wife, Ruth, served us a lunch of roast beef and mashed potatoes and corn and home-baked cherry pie; these are not people who live at a distance from their source of income.

McRae's home place is about ten air miles downwind from the open-pit mines and coal-fired electrical generating plants around an energy town called Colstrip. Miles of hilly grassland have been dug up by the great shovels; conveyor belts cross the horizons like something from a sci-fi dream. The perfect air is contaminated by sulfur dioxide and nitrogen dioxide (acid rain), and carbon dioxide (global warming).

Colstrip drove McRae and other farmers and ranchers, in 1972, to form the Northern Plains Resource Council, a populist movement that is the strongest environmental force in eastern Montana. They often stand against what is called progress (and jobs). In backland Montana that is understood as a radical position.

What they really are is deeply conservative. In such unlikely alliances, between environmentalists and traditionalists like McRae, we can begin to see the politics of our future.

Most of us in the West were brought up to believe the gifts of the world are to be used, but many of our ranchers and loggers, millworkers, miners are changing their minds. They are tired of seeing the mines and prairies and timber bought up by corporations and harvested for the enrichment of shareholders who live elsewhere. Never mind that they and people like them did the hands-on open-pit mining and timber-falling and cow-boying, they are shamed by clear-cut timberland hillslopes and saline seepage in the wheatfields and plowgrounds gone to dust, and silted, ruined trout streams. They have been rode hard, as the cowhand saying goes, and hung up wet.

But any new order is likely to be a long time coming; a lot of Montana people are still eager to sell their heritage.

Just east of the rockies front, near the white-man's community of Choteau (over a couple of hills from the outcropping where paleontologists found fossilized dinosaur eggs with baby duckbills inside), the Nature Conservancy owns an 18,000-acre tract called the Pine Butte Swamp Preserve. It is the last place where grizzlies come off the Rockies onto the plains (where they mostly lived before we drove them to the mountains). The centerpiece of the preserve is a 2,000-acre peatland known as a *fen* (swamp, except that the groundwater percolates through).

The fen is an intensely interwoven community of life (fifteen threatened species); it is at the spiritual and biological heart of a mixture of private and public lands along a 100-mile reach of the rockies front, which is the largest recovering game range in the world. Environmentalists want the rockies front declared wilderness; oil companies want it opened to drilling.

If the area is roaded it will no longer be eligible for wilderness designation; it will be developed. Pine Butte will be increasingly isolated from the front. The grizzlies will stop coming down from the mountains to the fen and the intricate flow of relationships in another biological community will have been irrevocably fractured.

Which would be fine with many people in Choteau; the grizzly have been known to kill cattle. And besides, "Think of the tax dollars. We could build a new library."

It's difficult to sympathize with them. The good citizens of Choteau look to be as well off as anybody in Montana; their eagerness to road the wild country seems to be driven mainly by greed.

You have to wonder if they really want the whole boom-town package, oil-field roughnecks with thousands of bucks a month spendable in their pockets, and the good times, cocaine and overloaded sewage systems and schools; you wonder if the folks in Choteau have consulted with old-timers around Evanston, Wyoming, or Wamsutter. The oil patch boomed down there about 1980. It lasted maybe three years.

But we're petroleum junkies. The game range along the rockies front has a good chance of turning out to be another national sacrifice area.

White people in the Northern Rockies have had the beaver trade and buffalo hunters, gold and silver, copper mines, homesteaders, boom times in lumber and petroleum, and each time we've ended up busted, looking for another way home.

In the long run national attention is likely to drive an agenda of severely restricting other than recreational uses of public lands, which are widely thought of as a national treasure (not treasure-house). If Westerners don't eventually take the initiative, and come up with a nationally acceptable program for public land use, they won't be calling the shots.

You just want to live in your own private Idaho.
—The B-52s

You take romance, I'll take jello.
—Ella Fitzgerald,
improvising on *"A Fine Romance"*

The principle supporting business now is rage.
—Richard Hugo,
"Degrees of Gray in Phillipsburg"

The American West has always been a double-hearted dream-land: a home in paradise, and a wide-open situation where you could maybe make a killing. Our economy has been historically based on a nineteenth-century public lands policy known as "multiple use" (subsidized timber, cheap grazing, minerals for the mining, free recreational access, a policy designed to encourage settlement and development). It has worked out, obviously, to be a sweet deal for the homefolks and an endless windfall for timber and mining corporations.

But all this is changing. Money men and power brokers are very much aware that the economic hot spots in the West are Reno (gambling), Las Vegas (gambling and defense), Salt Lake City (high-tech industry), Boise (computers), Aspen, Jackson Hole, and Santa Fe (amenities and recreation). Tourism and the educated are in the saddle, and they are going to be. Tourists come for the wilderness. They tend to despise the look of logging and mining (the missile silos are below ground and inconspicuous).

The old economic order in the West is right to fear environ-mentalists and others who understand the West as a place to be preserved, not used; the newcomers are going to prevail in the long run; they represent the will of the nation; they have de-mographics on their side. A majority of American citizens don't really care much about loggers and farmers and miners (or colonial economies like those in Montana and Wyoming). Rather, they care much more about preserving what's left of the natural world in the West, which in many cases they cor-rectly understand as theirs, for their own sweet recreational use.

The list of short-term cures for Montana's money problems is long as your leg: low-impact manufacturing, gambling (high-rise casinos along Flathead Lake), bilingual expeditions into the wilderness for the Germans and the Japanese, hunting enclaves with African-like safaris (up to $7,500 for a bull elk), Jack Nicklaus–designed golf resorts, helicopter skiing, writers and stockbrokers with their modems hooked up to New York and Los Angeles. We're in the process of inventing new ways to make a living, value added rather than extraction based, and it's sort of working. Experts say the economy in Montana is thriv-ing (we have a "good business atmosphere"). What this works out to mean is that Montana is at the moment a pretty good place to start up a business but a lousy place to work for wages.

What's new?

In old photographs we see sixty-seven loggers on the fresh-cut stump of a single ancient cedar tree, their long saws crossed, their sleeves rolled up—they stared into the camera like kings of the forest. They knew themselves in their work, but their work is vanishing. So far they have mostly stayed at their jobs and labored as colonials at what they love and know how to do. But they tell their kids to get educated and get out; they know their time is ending.

Our quintessential nineteenth-century Montana cowboy, Teddy Blue Abbott, once told Charlie Russell that he wished he had been born a hundred years earlier, as a Sioux Indian.

"They been living in heaven for a thousand years," Russell answered, "and we took it away from 'em for forty dollars a month."

You can catch the sadness unto death, and tire of white man dreams, and think you want to be an Indian. It is a way of leaving your troubles behind, and vanishing into some never-never land. Maybe even an old double-hearted trickster like Charlie Russell flirted with the idea.

It is a way of saying the best that can be is come and gone. Heroes inside mountain-man fantasies of their own invention parade our streets in buckskins and beads; Vietnam veterans still lurk in the high isolate lands near the tree line and the purity of wilderness. We had a famous case a few years ago; a couple of self-named mountain men, father and son, tried to kidnap a young woman to go live in the mountains with them, seemingly forever. It was their idea of beginning a new life. They were pilgrims, heading for the security of a make-believe past.

We've always been a shelter for crazies. And now a few anti-government nitwits are trying to terrorize some tiny little towns in northern Idaho and western Montana. They were drawn to the West by our open spaces and mythology of freedom. They think anything goes in the West. Some seem to yearn for martyrdom, and because of that, and their utter willingness to kill, are monstrously dangerous.

Some locals say Montana is becoming an out-West theme park. Our situation, they say, is rapidly going zoo-like, turning make-believe. Disneyland West is the way they think of it, Beverly Hills in the Highlands. They bemoan the fact that outsiders are buying their way in. Their grievances are no doubt partway an echo of old political lamentations about the division of spoils between the privileged and the poor. Saudis and Japanese and bi-coastal movie actors are buying up our prairies and saying we can't go hunting there any more. "Them rich people will lock up the gates like they was royalty from Europe," a man told me. "Where the hell will we get an elk?" There's some truth in the notion. But it's more than that—too many people, and this paradise will be gone forever, ruined, thronging and paved over.

Our distances are swarming with citizens devoted to stalking elk, and the chance of silence while osprey plunge after the kokanee out by the Bird Islands on Flathead Lake is virtually gone. Outside Sun Valley I saw a vast house being built to enclose an old weathered barn. I mean the whole barn was going to end up inside the living room. You could think of it as decor, a way of incorporating actuality into the dream.

A friend who lives on the Boulder River, south of Big Timber in central Montana, tells of being invited to a Christmas party by his neighbors, the CEO from San Francisco and his wife. My friend says he knew these people were rich, but didn't know the degree to which they'd made it count until he rang the doorbell, and was greeted by Jimmy Carter, a houseguest.

Best part, my friend says, it was no big deal. Here in the Rockies, lately, we've all got celebrity stories. We've been drawing rock stars, movie actors . . . Tom Brokaw, Liz Claiborne. If you're sitting in a restaurant in Bozeman and a guy at the next table is going on about Bob said this, and Bob did that, you can legitimately wonder if he's talking about Redford.

If he's talking about Ted and Jane, you don't have to wonder. Huey Lewis is on the board of a hospital in Missoula. Andie McDowell spends an occasional Saturday morning reading to children in Fact and Fiction, a Missoula bookstore. You meet screenwriters and cinematographers at the Circle K.

A friend tells of sitting beside a clean-featured young man in a blue-collar bar in Livingston. The talk got around to work. "What do you do?" my friend asked. "Movies," the young man said. "I'm a star." My friend turned the talk politely to other topics. Point is, he believed the young man's story. But he never did figure out which star.

The rich and famous mostly cluster in enclaves like Paradise Valley south of Livingston, where they settled on the heels of writer Thomas McGuane, a man with a genius for friendship and living well, who came around 1970= for the fishing, so he says= or nearby in the valley of the West Boulder River, or in the environs of Flathead Lake, or in the Bitterroot Valley south of Missoula. Real estate promoters like to claim Whitefish, a ski town at the north end of the Flathead Valley, is the next Aspen. Which, if you've ever been to Aspen, is sort of a joke. Whitefish has rather a long way to go. But, they say, Aspen wasn't much but a high-mountain ghost town at the end of World War II.

Through all this, the lament we continually hear is blame the rich strangers. It is a way of paralyzing ourselves.

To be fair, it's clear the more responsible of our most prosperous newcomers are drawn to Montana by more than faddism or connection with some kind of cowhand chic. They seem to find something in Montana that they take to be valuable— perhaps just life done in something like natural rhythms and scale. Some donate development rights on their properties to the Nature Conservancy or the Montana Land Reliance or Vital Ground. It is a way of practicing stewardship. They are to be congratulated.

It's not just the well-to-do. Seems like everybody is coming, a stream of vigorous retirees and nature-freaks and plain citizens on the lookout for possibilities. We've had our hundred years of solitude in the West.

The two-lane highway north past the beauties of the Sawtooth Mountains and the swales along the Salmon River, over Lost Trail Pass into the Bitterroot Valley, across the Clark Fork of the Columbia and past the Mission Mountains and Flathead Lake and Glacier Park to the blue Canadian Rockies, is all sort of (if the natural world does it for you) glorious. And it's a bumper-to-bumper raceway—Jeeps and Winnebagos and Harleys, Californians and Canadians, illicit drug vendors on holiday, fly-fishing nuts, who knows? Some of these hordes are tourists, but many are coming to stay. They've sold a house in some suburb, they're bringing what money they've got, and they're intent on buying in, souls on the run.

Who could blame them? Maybe they're interested in a life in connection with nature in some approximation of working order, or towns where children can be safe on the streets after school. Maybe they want to sleep with their doors unlocked and open to the summer night, or develop an ongoing relationship with a stretch of trout stream, going back to it over seasons until they know the runs and swirls better than they know the lines in their hands.

Up on the Big Blackfoot River we meet people who carry a copy of Norman Maclean's *A River Runs through It* while they cast to the water he wrote about. Some tell us they plan to move to Montana. We say no, the fishing has been ruined, forget it, stay home. We tell them lies but they come anyway.

Maybe they want to hike to lakes in the high mountains on Friday nights after work in the summertime, and drift to sleep while loons call in the moonlight. Maybe they want huge banks of white and purple lilac blooming beside their house in late spring, busy with hummingbirds.

Maybe they want to hunt pheasants along fence lines in the fall, or skiing in the immaculate wintertime mountains, or some simple talk about the beauty of things with neighbors they encounter in the barbershop. Maybe they want to take part in local politics with some clear sense their efforts could make a difference and feel they are living in a community with citizens who are well-intentioned toward one another.

On a flight out of Kalispell, I sat beside a big man in his fifties, a native with a bad limp he earned playing football for the Montana State Bobcats and riding in rodeos. He was moving to deepest Wyoming.

"There's nobody around here any more," he said, "but a bunch of golf course Canadians."

Many locals, the ones not selling real estate, are equally un-happy. Most of them like the money siphoning into the local economy, but they feel they're being invaded.

And they are. A lot of locals, former loggers and miners and such, are likely to end up in the servant business, employed as motel clerks and hunting guides, and they know it. It's not hard to figure why many people in the Rockies hate this wave of outlanders with such passion.

Imagine it. You've spent your life in a town by the river, where the cottonwood leaves flash in the evening breeze and you can leave your car unlocked on the streets. You can do a lit-tle fly-fishing at night after work or go for a run on a trail in the wilderness (the Rattlesnake Wilderness is just outside the city limits of Missoula). You hate seeing your paradise overrun by latecomers from some seaport. "I guess it's a trade," one fel-low told me. "We want the money, we got to put up with the ninnies."

"We can't afford to live here any more," people say, "not with the taxes."

Property taxes in some areas have tripled. Farmers near Kalispell can't afford to go on farming, and just twenty miles down the road at Eagle Bend, outlanders are paying several hundred thousand for a condo on the golf course. Some old-time Montana people feel they are fighting for their lives. They've generated a taxpayer's revolt.

A lot of newcomers are eager to join. Many are coming to the Rockies to retire. Their children are long out of school. They're on fixed incomes, and resist supporting education.

A bumper sticker says, IF YOU THINK EDUCATION IS EXPENSIVE, TRY IGNORANCE. But these good folks don't seem to give a damn about the welfare of our next generation. They want to buy into our functioning culture on the cheap. And it seems to be working out for them.

What's drawing these crowds? Ultimately, I think, it's not so much the beauties of nature, or cheap land and houses, as it is safety. Sanctuary.

Out in the great society (California, the East), as we know, our old America fantasy—a new world and social justice all around—has gone seriously defunct. Millions of citizens in our cities quite justifiably count themselves disenfranchised. Some are angry, armed, and dangerous.

So much fear is shredding the webwork of affection and responsibility that is at the heart of any good society. Many people are dropping everything, leaving the cities, running.

Is this the old dream, America the beautiful, and I want my share? Is this all that's left of the dream, a hideout in the Rockies, the last safe place? Maybe, except for certain locals, who are also armed and furious.

One warm afternoon in October I walked under the great western red cedar in the Ross Cedar Tree Grove, a remnant of modified Pacific Maritime forest in western Montana. Tamarack were dropping their golden needles on the mountains, cottonwood were blooming vivid yellow along the Bull River. I hated people who want to harvest one of the main reasons we have for living here (call it beauty), and could not stop myself.

I despised my anger.

It was an indulgence, a form of foolishness. We must learn to step on our own anger. Issues of fairness, privilege, and class resonate through our history. Much of our discontent has been generated by our ongoing story about the wealthy against the working stiffs.

If we're ever going to quit reliving that story in Montana and the West we have to talk things out, searching for accord, however difficult and long-winded the undertaking. We need to recognize that adversarial, winner-take-all, showdown political decision-making is a way we defeat ourselves. Our future starts when we begin honoring the dreams of our enemies while staying true to our own.

We need to invent a new story for ourselves, in which we live in a society that understands killing the natural world as a way of killing each other. It will be a story in which we acknowledge that the institutionalization of social and economic injustices is a way of doing the same thing.

We need a story in which the processes of communality and mutual responsibility are fundamental. We need to figure out how many populations we have, try to name their dreams, and begin resolving those dreams into a societal agenda for the future. It would seem reasonable to expect our politicians to take the lead in such processes, but they don't; they don't seem capable.

We need to take our politics back from the lawyers and the professionals and the boys with money (this is true, clearly, at every level in our democracy). If we can work our way through to public consensus the bureaucrats and lawmakers will follow.

Then, maybe, in Montana, we'll be able to decide, in some responsible way, what we want for our coal and oil (if we want to sell), and which is timberland and which is wilderness, and where the grizzlies should live, and the wolves, the buffalo and the elk (if we want them at all), and where to find the money to care for our poor and our disoriented and our disabled and our dispossessed (the Native Americans, at least, however extensive their reservations), and repair our decaying highways. And, most fundamentally, how to pay for first-rate schools (our main economic hope in any long run).

A lot of people came to the West and found a secure life and saw their values written into law, over generations. My father found an untouched place; he got the first shot at it; he inherited an old story: Take charge, make it pay. Our problems now are much more complex. We are responsible for imagining our way into a just society, and an economy based on our own labor and inventiveness rather than continued deep plowing in the pastures of heaven.

4

Some of us dream we are witnessing the birth of a heartland nation in the American West; an empire that runs down the spine of the continent from the blue Canadian Rockies to the cowboy kingdoms of Wyoming and the Colorado plateau, and beyond to the ski-lift highlands above Durango and Santa Fe, at the edge of southwestern deserts where the Hopi and citizens at Acoma built their cities on the mesa-tops (in the sky), which remind us of how good we could be.

In 1805 one of our first wayfarers in the West, Meriwether Lewis, sat beguiled beside the thunderous falls of the Missouri River (since dammed for hydroelectric power) and told himself this West was not only the great useful place Jefferson had instructed him to discover and treasure for the republic, but it was also sublime—by which he likely meant it reeked of obscurity, privation, vacuity, solitude, silence, boundlessness, and thus, of almost infinite possibility. As it still sort of does.

The dusty herds, the drifts of wild-eyed longhorn cattle moved north from Texas. But we don't encounter much in the way of actual livestock any more except in the deep heart of the off-the-Interstate in the West, where hardly nobody goes. Lonesome snoose-spitting buckaroos are a rare item.

What we mostly see in our travels are empty-eyed plastic

Herfords grazing our abstract *turista* realities. They are in-
tended, we imagine, to promote fellowship, and country-man
Jeffersonian virtues, meat-eating and dairy products. Or what?
The signs say EAT!

Those great make-believe cattle are calm, tame, domesticated, a hollow species; they echo of their hollowness if you
slap them with your hand, or bounce a brick off them. Shot
with a rifle, by country men on a tear, they just go on standing,
defaced but not at all wounded.

They are nothing if not amiable. Why do we so despise
them?

Maybe it's because they are so much like us, and emblem-
atic of so many insults we suffer. In them we see pastoral life in
its excellence—honeybees in the alfalfa while we idle on the
sandy bank of a little creek—reduced to an advertisement, a try
at cultivating another clot of false desire in the beholder, a
yearning to be Western. As in, "Gee, maybe if I stopped by the
plastic cow and had a rib steak and a milkshake I wouldn't feel
so hollow and crazy."

It was late afternoon when I sat in the bar in Lathrop Wells,
trying to get myself over to knock on the door at a bordello
called "The Valley of the Dolls." I was doing research on local
Nevada attitudes toward the proposed nuclear dump. But I really didn't want to know what the whorehouse people thought
about the dangerous business of selling yourself. I'd already
heard the jokes about radioactive, glowing genitalia. I wanted to
listen to a story in which nobody is tempted into making any
deals with the devil.

So I left those women to their lives, and drove back to my
motel. On my way south from Montana I'd driven through

fifty-mile slants of storm sweeping down from the great snow-bright spine of the Ruby Mountains in central Nevada, and dreamed of explorers in the New World, Jedediah Smith and his companions, horseback and alone in the spring of 1827, the first white men to traverse the Great Basin. I was dumbfounded in my pleasure as I toyed with the idea that all of us on the highway were explorers as we traveled into such beauties and long desolations.

Around noon I turned east from Ely, toward Great Basin National Park, which President Reagan signed into being in 1986. It is possible to understand Great Basin as Reagan's gift to his friend Paul Laxalt—or as a kind of sop to the people of Nevada, a way of making up for the continued devastation of their lands. I wanted to visit the Bristlecone Pine, the oldest living thing on earth. But the roads to Wheeler Peak were snowed shut. So I visited the Lehman Caves instead.

The Park Ranger told a story about the Bristlecone Pine. A researcher was trying to count the tree rings and set a maximum age for the Bristlecone. And he was having trouble with his core drill. So he took a chainsaw to what he thought to be the oldest tree on the mountain. And it worked; he killed the oldest thing living on earth in order to count its years.

Our species, I think, is emotionally hard-wired to every so often hit some road. Richard Hugo said, "The car that brought you here still runs."

There come times, like midsummer, when we yearn for nights of dancing with strangers. We find ourselves overwhelmed by the intricacies of our household arrangements, maybe swamped by what a friend once called "the bastard unfairness of things." The cure involves a getaway. We are by nature, I think, not entirely at ease with nonstop domesticity.

The Aboriginal people of Australia had themselves a sweet dream: travel, and as you travel, sing of the world as you see it in its luminous intricacy, bringing it into being. Think of the ancient child riding on its mother's hip, listening as she walks on through the endless world, speaking the names of things, inventing the actual for her child: teal, badger, skull, moon, ocotillo, roadrunner.

I want to spend some time loafing with the horny toads. I want to say, as the hot day cools and twilight settles over the upland Sonoran deserts of the southwest, "Double martini, Bombay, very dry and bitterly chilled, up."

Interstate 15 connects the past and present Empire Cities on the western side of the Rockies—Butte, Salt Lake City, and Las Vegas (and the megopolis that no doubt rules our future in the interior West, Los Angeles). We find it a good idea to tip a nod to memories of St. Patrick's Day on the streets of Butte, and pass on. We were younger then. Annick and I stay the night in Salt Lake City so we can visit Kurt Oberhansley at his Cafe Santa Fe in Emigration Canyon. We eat spectacular food, and make first contact with our nightly martini. This is absolutely and at last *the road.*

The next day, south of Cedar City, Interstate 15 drops off the highlands of central Utah. *Calm down, look around.*

It's important to get off the Interstate. Nobody has Vegas in mind. I sort of love the Mirage—white tigers, orchids, floor girls tipping you the wink—but it's life inside a computer game. I'm yearning for meaningful interaction with the actual.

Fortunately, Zion is at hand. The asphalt trail along the North Fork of the Virgin River is thronging with hundreds of tourists, but the air is invisible. You can taste this clarity while climbing up to imagine sailing off over the precipitous red-rock world.

All I have to do is breathe and see. My semi-Buddhist friends tell me to attempt vanishing into the breathing and into the seeing. I could do the same thing, Annick tells me, down by Bear Creek, studying the water-striders, a half-mile from her log house in Montana. But I'm listening to another voice.

This, it whispers, *is it*. I'm awake.

By late afternoon we've made our way over the forested highlands of the Kaibab Plateau, down to the long flats of House Rock Valley. The Vermillion Cliffs are a great stone reef adrift in twilight ocher. We'll stay tonight in the fisherman's motel near the edge of Marble Canyon, and make our meal on fresh-baked trout and homemade macaroni and cheese served by a Navajo woman who sighs and sings a little song in some language of her own as she brings our apple pie.

After breakfast amid fishermen, we drop down to the launch ramp at Lee's Ferry. Annick likes to imagine running the Grand Canyon at least once in her life (and we will, by the time you read this we will have done it—pray for me, a desert boy who can't swim the length of his automobile). I'm interested in the life and fate of John Doyle Lee, leader of the Mountain Meadows Massacre.

In the hard summer of 1857 a wagon train bound for southern California came down through the settlements of Utah, mostly living off food they stole from the locals. This drove the impoverished settlers to set an ambush and kill them (all but those children too young to remember). After that terrible day, our man John Doyle Lee retired to run the ferry deep in this canyon, where he lived with his family until he was tried in Cedar City, decades later, and shot by a firing squad.

That's a short version of his story.

Lee's house and orchard are still there. I keep a withered limb I found under one of his pear trees to remind me of the disasters we can create in response to true belief. I wish someone would murmur words like *irony* and *humor*. But no such luck. I'm left to pull up my own socks. As the poet Mary Oliver wrote, "There is only one question: How to love this world."

The names resonate once we get past the abominable dam holding back the abominable reservoir above Page, Arizona—Navajo names: Kaibito, Shonto, Betatakin, Kayenta, Chilchinbito. We're onto the plateau that was home to the so-called ancient people, the Anasazi. Off south over the curve of earth the Hopi live in their villages, without us, in what seems a coherent relationship to sacredness. In other years we've walked the paths between the old houses on Second Mesa, gazing away to horizons, and wondered what's wrong with us, why couldn't this kind of life be enough, why do we keep on trucking? Are we only driven by an excess of make-believe? Who, we decided, knows? Then we drove south to Sedona, and some Merlot and mesquite-fired lamb chops while the sliver of yellow moon hung belly-down in the purple night.

Every year or so Annick and I park on the south side of Canyon de Chelly, where the White House lives, and make our way down the cliffside path to fields at the bottom where the

Navajo tended thousands of peach trees until Kit Carson's men cut them down in the last century. It was a way of defeating the Navajo.

We tie plastic sacks over our shoes and wade sandbar to sandbar across the little creek in ankle-deep water. We time it so we can be alone and hear breathing, which is in one sense only the sigh of winds over the vast face of water-stained rock above us. Annick says she once heard bells.

The White House is a few decaying mud-brick rooms on a rocky shelf in that enormous cliff, the most stunningly situated human habitation I have witnessed. You wonder at the courage and wit of people so devoted to beauty they would live perched on a precipice where their children could fall off. Or were they driven to it?

What did lifetimes in such a place do to them? Were they more attuned to the utter fundament of things than we are, or did the splendor of their surroundings remind them too directly of their own fragilities? Why did they leave? Would the stony majesty of these cliffs, hovering over the fertile bottoms, over years, remind you too insistently of your own mortality? I can't see much beyond myself.

In France, Annick and I wandered over the limestone ridges along the Vezere River in the Dordogne, and took a guided walk into one of the caves decorated some twenty thousand years ago by people who must have been something like the people who lived in the White House, and even us in their willingness to attempt loving the world.

The cave, outside a village called Les Eyzies and a dozen kilometers from Lascaux, was called Font de Guame. The image that stunned us was of two reindeer: the female was on her knees and the male was licking at her lips as if in adoration.

It was an image important enough to be inscribed on a rough wall several hundred yards into the absolute darkness of a narrow cavern by people who seem to have understood, as we must, that holiness involves our fundamental impulse to love the world and care for it. It was another wake-up call.

We walk the Anasazi ruins in Chaco Canyon, fingering at the intricately stacked stony balustrades of Bonita Pueblo under a blazing sky. But we've brought our uptown uneasiness with us. Not a thing seems right except the notion of parrot feathers some anthropologists found as they excavated these sites. Miracles from the south, so vividly green, news from another way of yearning. What's wrong?

William Eastlake lived in the hills of northern New Mexico, off to the east near the little town of Cuba, while he wrote *Bronc People* and *Portrait of the Artist with Twenty-Six Horses*, work that should have rewarded him with every prize they make. He said New Mexico was too isolated, too quiet. He said it drove him to dreams of wildness. I know what he meant.

Maybe too domesticated means one-dimensional, as in Herefords and the suburbs. At least Eastlake got the work done before he pulled up and left. We're bound for Santa Fe. We have a casita reserved. After an early-evening nap we can amble over to the dark barroom and make a late meal on dainties. We'll eat nothing but famous snacks, smoked salmon, huge shrimp, melted brie and the tentacles of deep-fried squid.

We wake to laziness. It's a day to forego agendas, and read.

A book to travel with is Lewis Hyde's *The Gift*, which in its intelligence and generosity of spirit *is* a gift. Hyde quotes Czeslaw Milosz: "The smell of winter apples, of hoarfrost, and of linen. There are nothing but gifts on this poor, poor earth."

We drift through rooms hung with Georgia O'Keefe paintings in the museum on the square, we visit the traditional villages of Chimayo (I bought a rug from the weavers) and Truchas (where Redford shot some of *The Milagro Beanfield War*—the only evidence of that disruption is a sign reading MILAGRO GAS).

We see Georgia O'Keefe's patterns on the hills as we head down to the Rio Grande (imagining a black automobile parked at the roadside, and a woman at her painting). The streets of Los Alamos are too orderly (as Richard Hugo said of another small western town, "laid out by the insane"). We solace ourselves with a visit to Bandelier, where ancient inhabitants carved their dwellings into the soft-stone cliffs.

The next morning we drive on to the sky-city of Acoma (where I buy Annick a fine silver necklace). Is this the right way to proceed, driving and buying? We encounter a gila monster out on the fourth fairway at Troon North, outside Phoenix, the old animal scuttling toward cover in the bush. Maybe I'm not escaping into much but the artificiality of myself, which is always the danger.

Where were you last night?

Out.

What were you running from?

Civilization, I want to say, and one of its prime discontents, which might be called the Stuck on the Wheel of Repetition

Disorder, or Boredom unto Temporary Blindness. We've decided to head for the coast. We're ready for the feel of firm sand under our bare feet as we walk the beach and keep pace with dolphins as they surface and resurface in the breakers offshore. Last February we went out to Anacapa Island off Santa Barbara and saw gray whales and elephant seals and the brilliant yellow Coreopsis in bloom, pelicans and cormorants.

This time we'll spend days out there beneath the rocky seacliffs, in the tide pools. We'll slow down. Maybe I'll learn to *see* again, like a child. My senses will begin to open out. It's easy to look at photographs and imagine red crabs and purple sea urchins. But who knows what we'll really find as we relearn arts of witnessing miracles, and miracles? These are some of the names: Rockweed, sea kelp, surf grass, murrelet. These are my reasons for travel.

We run to the night and the highlands and the sea, to sports and whiskey and work and whatever else, most often as a way of fleeing to territory where we might forget our insistent home-town selves. Such journeying is not altogether indulgence. It's necessary, every so often, to reawaken our love of things.

Don't mistake me. I believe deeply in the virtues of communal life. It's just that, like agriculture, they can be practiced too intensively.

5

Annick and I were shuffling through the reefs of fallen leaves in luminous October light, heading for our yearly football game in the little stadium at the University of Montana above the Clark Fork River in Missoula. We exchange shouts with three writers and some old downtown drinking cronies, and talked shop with Dan Flores, the environmental historian. I rubbed shoulders with a famous rock-and-roll musician in the hot-dog line; it all led me to feel I was at one with what I'd chosen in life.

Some of the sweetest times, for me, are warm afternoons when the autumn sky is blue-white and infinite in its distance from our concerns. Cottonwood along the rivers bloom huge and pale yellow against the evergreen mountains, and we will never grow old, our people will never die. No one will break into our house while we're gone. A long winter is coming. We'll embrace it if we have any brains, ski, roll in the snow. Or not (I, in my witless way, head south).

At the football game we rooted for our team, and won. If my happiness about that seems excessively stupid, and I can understand that it might, I'm not very sorry. When we got home my front door was standing open but nothing was touched. Maybe it was the wind.

In Asia people save themselves from sorrow by meditating

on a paradise of their own inventing, which they call the Pure Land. Attempting to see each swirl in the river, leaves on the mountain slope, each intricate butterfly in the sun, they try to find peace in the creature they are. In spring the purple and white lilac will blossom in enormous clots of splendor along the alleyways in Missoula.

If the weather holds we could live forever. Or anyway give it a try. *Momento vivere.*

EPILOGUE

Doing Good Work Together
The Politics of Storytelling

Plot in fiction helps us overcome the anxiety caused by the loss of the "sacred masterplot" that organizes and explains the world. Our lives are ceaselessly intertwined with narrative, with the stories that we tell or hear told, those that we dream or imagine or would like to tell, all of which are reworked in that story of our own lives that we narrate to ourselves in an episodic, somewhat semiconscious, but virtually uninterrupted monologue. We live immersed in narrative . . .

= Peter Brooks, *Reading for the Plot*

As they are told and retold, stories have the function of wrestling with the ultimately inexplicable chaos of reality around us. They give it form, and in shaping and reshaping the form, they help us gain control over it.

= interview with Alan Jabbour of the National Folklife Center

The poet C.K. Williams came to Missoula some years ago, and

spoke of "narrative dysfunction" as a prime part of mental illness in our time. Many of us, he said, lose track of the story of
ourselves, the story that tells us who we are supposed to be and
how we are supposed to act.

It isn't any fun, and it doesn't just happen to people, it happens to entire societies. Stories are places to live, inside the
imagination. We know a lot of them, and we're in trouble when
we don't know which one is ours. Or when the one we inhabit
doesn't work any more, and we stick with it anyway.

We live in stories. What we are is stories. We do things because of what is called *character*, and our character is formed by
the stories we learn to live in. Late in the night we listen to our
own breathing in the dark, and rework our stories. We do it
again the next morning, and all day long, before the looking
glass of ourselves, reinventing reasons for our lives. Other than
such storytelling there is no reason for things.

Aristotle talks of "recognitions," which can be thought of as
moments of insight or flashes of understanding in which we
see through to coherencies in the world. We are all continually
seeking after such experiences. It's the most commonplace
thing human beings do after breathing. We are like detectives,
each of us trying to make sense and define what we take to be
the right life. It is the primary, most incessant business of our
lives.

We figure and find stories, which can be thought of as maps
or paradigms in which we see our purposes defined; then the
world drifts and our maps don't work any more, our paradigms
and stories fail, and we have to reinvent our understandings,
and our reasons for doing things. Useful stories, I think, are
radical in that they help us see freshly. They are like mirrors, in

which we see ourselves reflected. That's what stories are for, to help us see for ourselves as we go about the continual business of reimagining ourselves.

If we ignore the changing world, and stick to some story too long we are likely to find ourselves in a great wreck. It's happening all over the West, right now, as so many of our neighbors attempt to live out rules derived from old models of society that simply reconfirm their prejudices.

They get to see what they want to see. Which is some consolation. But it is not consolation we need. We need direction.

The interior West is no longer a faraway land. Our great emptiness is filling with people, and we are experiencing a time of profound transition, which can be thought of as the second colonization. Many are being reduced to the tourist business, in which locals feature as servants, hunting guides and motel maids, or local color. People want to enclose our lives in theirs, as decor.

The Native American people were living coherent lives, at one with their circumstances, when our people displaced them, leaving them mostly disenfranchised and cut off from possibility in our society, their reservations like little beleaguered nations battling to survive in our larger one as we continue wrecking the traditional resources of their cultures. The result, for them, is anomie, nothing to hang onto, powerlessness. We are shamed and look away, and do little to help.

So it is deeply ironic that the Native Americans are being joined in their disenfranchisement by loggers and miners and ranchers, and the towns that depend on them. Our ancestors came to the West and made homes for themselves, where they could live independent lives. Because of their sacrifices, we in the dominant society think we own the West, we think they earned it for us. But, as we know, nobody owns anything absolutely, except their sense of who they are.

One Sunday, while living in the heart of the French Quarter of New Orleans, Annick and I were out walking in the rain when we realized we were hearing the echoes of someone singing, a vivid, unaccompanied voice in the narrow street, maybe three blocks away when I first heard her, a black woman with her eyes closed and face lifted to the mist as her voice rose and fell to *Glory, Glory, Halleluljah.*

She shone in the gray light. I almost couldn't look, and wondered if she cared what anybody thought as I dropped two folded paper dollars into the coffee can at her feet. She didn't look at me at all.

Semitropical plants were draped along the lacy ironwork balconies above the broken sidewalk, nature in a place where everything was carpentered. My shuttered door was one in a wall of shuttered doors that stretched on toward Bourbon Street, each painted thick, deep green. The light seemed to rebound from the walls, illuminating the wet bricks.

I can still hear that woman. Her life looked to be endlessly more difficult than mine. Her courage and passion were evident in singing even if it was a street shuck for money, and I envied her. I felt like weeping, for myself, and I was afraid of it, like something in my body might break.

There I was, living nearby to some of the best eating and drinking and music in the world, in a place where I never heard so many people—black, white, creole, cajun—laughing so much of the time, and I was awash with sadness.

Maybe it was because I had never lived so close to so much violence, which was the other side of things. During Mardi Gras, on Rampart Street, a little more than three blocks from our door, some lost tourist was shot every night, killed and robbed, mainly for drug money. Every week or so there was a schoolyard killing, a kid assassinating another kid with a handgun, settling scores.

The perpetrators in these crimes were most often young men from the so-called projects, publicly owned housing for the poor. Those young men were alienated and angry because they saw correctly that their situation in society was hopeless—they were essentially uneducated, their schools were war zones, and their chances of finding jobs, much less meaningful and respected work, were nil. A friend who grew up in New Orleans said, "They've got no place to go. There's no ladder up, no ladder out. They're left with nothing but selfishness. It's the second lesson you learn on the streets." The first lesson, according to my friend, is that nothing, nobody, is bulletproof.

It might be useful for us in the West to consider the ways in which the projects in New Orleans, in their capacity to generate hopelessness, are much like so many of our failing towns and our Indian Reservations. It might be instructive to consider the rage that is generated by such disenfranchisement, and think of the ways it looks when it gets to the streets of our cities; it might be instructive to look closely at various riots in Los Angeles.

It starts with broken promises. In the West, people came thinking they had been promised something, at least freedom and opportunity, and the possibility of inventing a new, fruitful life. That was the official mythology. When that story didn't come true, the results were alienation, and anomie, just like in the projects, just like in L.A.

When people are excluded from what their society has defined for them as the main rewards of life, when they sense that they are absolutely out of the loop, as a lot of Americans do in the rural outback and in the deep heartlands of the cities, they sometimes turn to heedless anger.

A lot of people on our streets are staring back at us (the enfranchised) with hatred that we all know to be at least partway justifiable. Some among them, we can see, might kill us for our selfishness. Fewer and fewer of them are willing to stand singing in the rain, waiting for a few dollars to accumulate in the tin can at their feet.

Many of us live with a sense that there is something deeply and fundamentally wrong in our society. Many of us feel our culture has lost track of the reasons one thing is more significant than another. We are fearful and driven to forget the most basic generosities. We anesthetize ourselves with selfishness. It's not, we say, *our* fault.

Many of us live insulated, as I do much of the time. In New Orleans I liked to walk down a couple of blocks to the Bombay Club and disassociate my sensibilities with one and then another huge perfect martini. In Las Vegas I like to stay at the brilliantly named Mirage, amid those orchids and white tigers. What I don't like to do is walk the streets and look the other side of my society in the eye.

I want to think I deserve what I get. I don't want to consider how vastly I am overrewarded. I don't want to consider the in-

justices around me. I don't want any encounters with the disenfranchised. I want to say it is not my fault.

But it is, it's mine, and ours. We'd better figure out ways to
spread some equity around if we want to go on living in a society that is at least semi-functional. It's a fundamental responsibility, to ourselves.

We inhabit a complex culture that is intimately connected
to societies all over the world, vividly wealthy while increasingly polarized between rich and poor, increasingly multiethnic
and multiracial, predominately urban, sexually ambiguous,
ironic, self-reflexive, drug-crazied, dangerous, and resounding
with discordant energies—a selfish, inhumane society without
a coherent myth to inhabit, a society coming unglued, a democracy that is failing. Its citizens do not believe in it any more,
they don't vote, they withdraw from the processes of governing
themselves. On C-Span, all day long, you will see the other end
of that same society, privileged, long-faced citizens trying to
figure out what to do about our trouble without foregoing their
privileges. You will see a society without much idea how to proceed.

I want to inhabit a story in which the animals all lay down
with one another, everybody satisfied, children playing on
sandy beaches by a stream, in the warm shade of the willows
the flash of salmon in the pools. Children of your own as you
see them. How do we understand our kingdom?

It is easy to see the world is luminous with significances.
We want them to be part of the story of our life, the most important characters after ourselves. We yearn to live in a coherent place we can name, where we can feel safe. We want that

place to exist like a friend, somebody we can know. What we need most urgently, in both the West and all over America, is a fresh dream of who we are, which will tell us how we should act, a set of stories to reassure us in our sense that we deserve to be loved. We want the story of our society to have a sensible plot. We want it to go somewhere, we want it to mean something.

We must define some stories about taking care of what we've got, which is to say life and our lives. They will be stories in which our home is sacred, stories about making use of the place where we live without ruining it, stories that tell us to stay humane amid our confusions.

We must define a story that encourages us to understand that the living world cannot be replicated. We hear pipe dreams about cities in space, but it is clearly impossible to replicate the infinite complexities of the world in which we have evolved. Wreck it and we will have lost ourselves, and that is craziness. We are animals evolved to live in the interpenetrating energies and subjectivities of all the life there is, so far as we know, life that coats the rock of earth like moss. We cannot live without connection, both psychic and physical. We begin to die of pointlessness when we are isolated, even if some of us can hang on for a long while connected to nothing beyond our imaginations.

We need to inhabit stories that encourage us to pay close attention, we need stories that will encourage us toward acts of the imagination that in turn will drive us to the arts of empathy, for each other and the world. We need stories that will encourage us to understand that we are part of everything, the world exists under our skins, and destroying it is a way of killing ourselves. We need stories that will drive us to care for one another and the world. We need stories that will drive us to take action.

One spring evening Annick and I went to stand with the other tourists beneath the glass-bottomed fish ladder in the Seattle Aquarium. We could see up through the clear glass and clean water to salmon suspended amid the sunset clouds and the first glinting of stars, those fish returning to spawn at the head of that fish ladder where they had hatched. It was all artifice, stupid and manipulative, except for the urge to return that those salmon carried in their genes, heart-breaking in its precision and beauty.

Out on the coasts of the Pacific Northwest I gaze into the intricate complexity of a pool uncovered by the lowering tide, and a light wind from the southwest brings the stink of the sea, and I look up to see the steely orange slant of light from the low sun converging with the gray slants of rain out beyond the oriental look of certain offshore rocky seastacks crowned with an edge of evergreen, and I am inhabiting a dream of the right life. Like a bed where a child has been recently made, our best places reek of fecundity; we want to live in situations that encourage us to experience such coherencies.

On the headland beyond Neah Bay, at the most western extremity of the Pacific Northwest, Annick and I watched black-and-white killer whales cruise south through breaking seas. Then we spent some afternoon hours in the rain with our separate tribes of children and my grandchildren on the beaches south of La Push, knocking mussels off the seastack rocks. We steamed the mussels for our dinner while our wool socks steamed by the fire, and we got into dry clothes and sniffed the gin cap and the rain went on falling outside in the twilight.

On a cloudless evening my grown-up children took us sailing on Lake Washington, with the towers of Seattle lighted to the south of us. It was more of perfection than we deserved, I had to think, while not so far away, in terms of air travel, babies were starving.

Too much order and artificiality makes us crazy.

The feel of mud where the leeches breed, as it oozes around my ankles, and osprey fishing with their killing clarity of purpose, rot on the evening breeze, all the stink and predatory swiftness of things, they are part of what I understand as most valuable. We are born to messes.

The seacoasts can be heart-stopping in their natural beauty, a melding of aspects both actual and imagined, drawing us to intuit that the world does not proceed in a haphazard manner. Heaven is a fiction we construct around real places, a way of imagining that says my time and stories are not meaningless.

I am in my sixth decade of life, my friends are dying, people of my generation, and I have still not come to anything like a set of consolations for my own fragility.

This is no joking matter. I am irreligious as a stone, and no more profound or coherent in my thinking about such matters than I was at age eleven. Let it go, I thought (at eleven), there's plenty of time, you'll think of something.

But no such luck. Soon enough I am going to have my chance. It's time to lay hands on a sustaining mythology. If I were dying, would I be inconsolable? How do you get consolable? I tell myself I had better find a way.

So I examine my beliefs, if they were beliefs—they felt more like dreams. What a peculiar thing, examining beliefs.

There is no methodology. Beliefs are like air; they are not justifiable; they are the medium we live in.

What do you believe? I question myself. You don't need reasons, I tell myself, and I discover (I think I discover; maybe this is a story I invented in the act of that attempt at discovering) that what I believe is simpleminded and positive and that it derives from memories of childhood and nature. Way back then I understood that the apparent world resonates with all the meaning there is ever going to be.

We need stories that tell us reasons why taking care, why compassion and the humane treatment of our fellows is more important—and interesting—than feathering our own nests as we go on accumulating property and power. Our lilac bloom, and buzz with honeybees and hummingbirds. We can still find ways to live in some approximation of home-child heaven. There is no single, simple story that will define paradise for us and never will be. As we know, the world will not stand still, energies and processes are what is actual, complexity is actual.

On summer mornings I can walk down Higgins Avenue to the Farmer's Market by the old Great Northern Depot in Missoula, and buy baby carrots and white daisies, zinnias, snow peas, new corn, gladiola, iris, and chard. In my simple-minded way I love the old men selling long-stemmed roses, and the hippie mothers who are becoming farm wives. I try to imagine their secrets.

When I buy, I like to deal with the Hmong, refugees from the highlands of Laos. They have been in Montana since the end of hostilities in Vietnam. They were relocated courtesy of the CIA, their cohorts in the narcotics trade, at least that's the story we were told. I wonder if their old people are crazy with grief for lost villages. Maybe they are, or maybe they were glad to escape.

On the wall above the place where I write there is a bed-spread embroidered by a Hmong woman, imaginary animals on a field of tropical green, a royal red elephant with black ears, a turtle with a yellow-and-blue-and-red checkered shell, a blackrabbit, an orange monkey on a branch, a parrot, a peacock, and a green prehistoric creature with white horns. It is the work of a woman transported a long way from her homeland, who stayed tough enough to dream up another story. It gives me heart.

WILLIAM KITTREDGE grew up on the MC Ranch in southeastern Oregon, where he lived until he was thirty-five. His books include *Hole in the Sky*, *Owning It All*, and *We Are Not in This Together*. He now teaches at the University of Montana.